Nutsucker

1st Edition

COLLIN J. RAE

ISBN: 979-8-9885957-6-2

Illustrations and cover design by Collin J. Rae

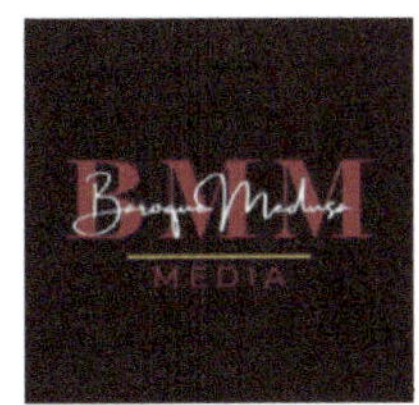

Intro

Above all this is a book about cruelty.
The cruelty we inflict on ourselves.
The cruelty we inflict on others.
The cruelty we perceive as being inflicted upon us.
The cruelty we see every day and feel powerless to stop.
Accidental cruelty.
Peripheral cruelty.
The cruelty in us.
The cruelty around us.
That glorious cruelty of being.
That devastating cruelty of just being.
All-consuming cruelty.
And it's aftermath.

"It does not mean what you think it means" - Kristine Snodgrass

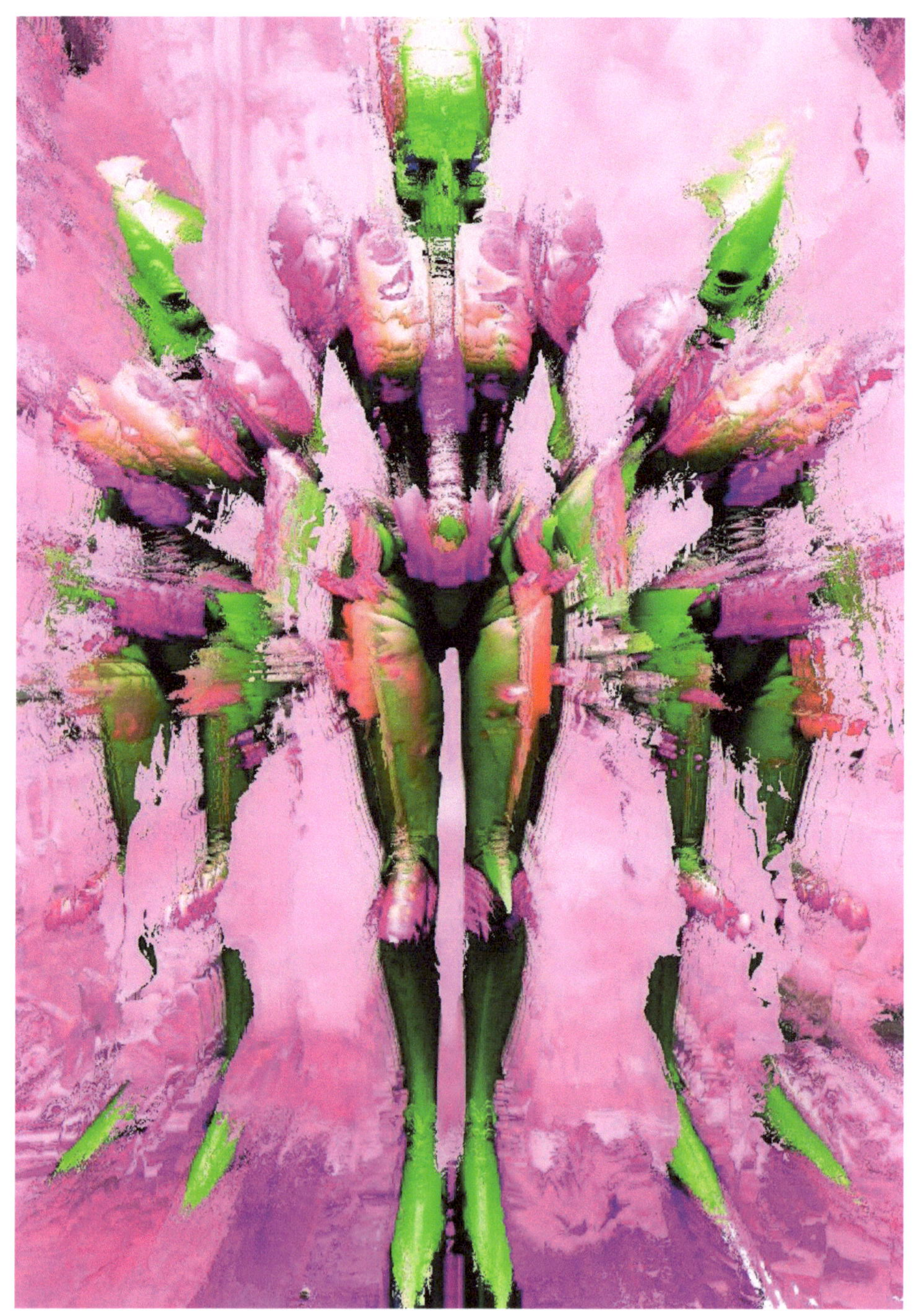

The Morbid History of a Slow Slurp

My words are a crime against you
obliterated by luminous brain-scapes
sorting the used and the useless
into mountains of random refuge
your history is a dime-store condom
an armless punk in fucked flame
in league with your liars leer.

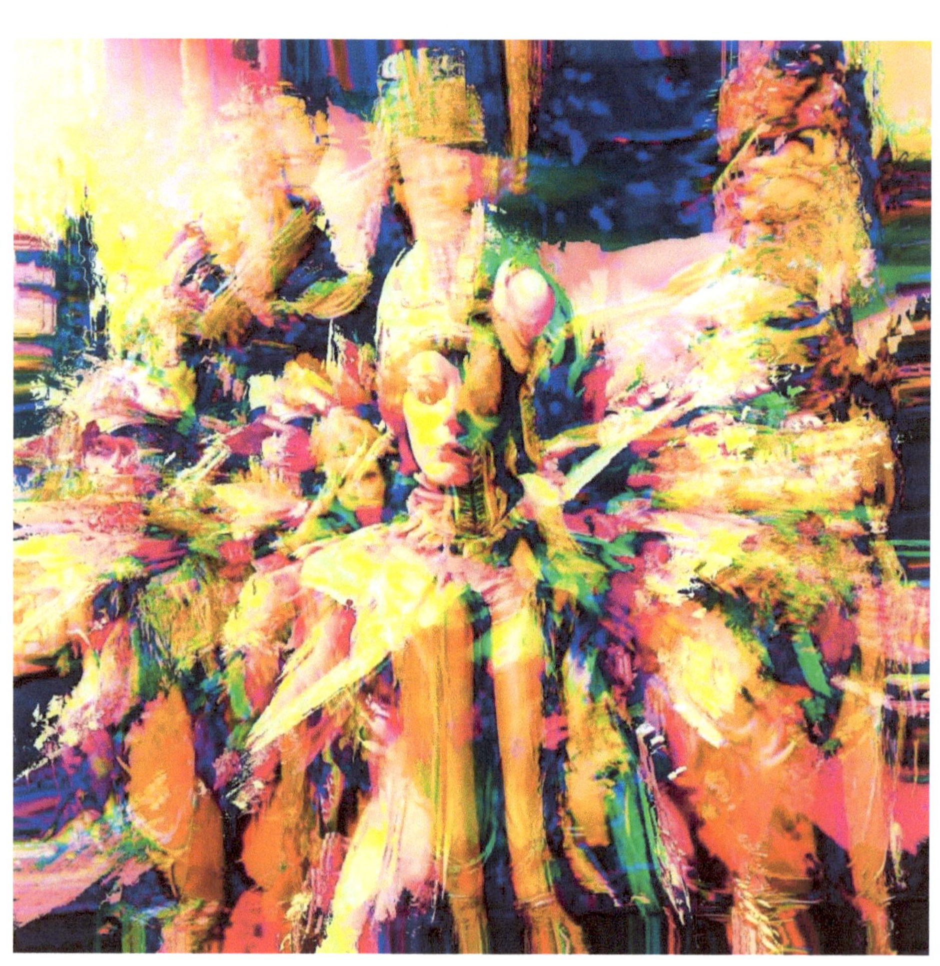

Grief and a Broken Fuckhead

No forward no backward
a memoir of shit based sarcasm
burrowed in blank eyes
the erotic nature of ghosts
and gorotic tenure
tragic is your guts in flames
on this day of severe incendiary reflection.

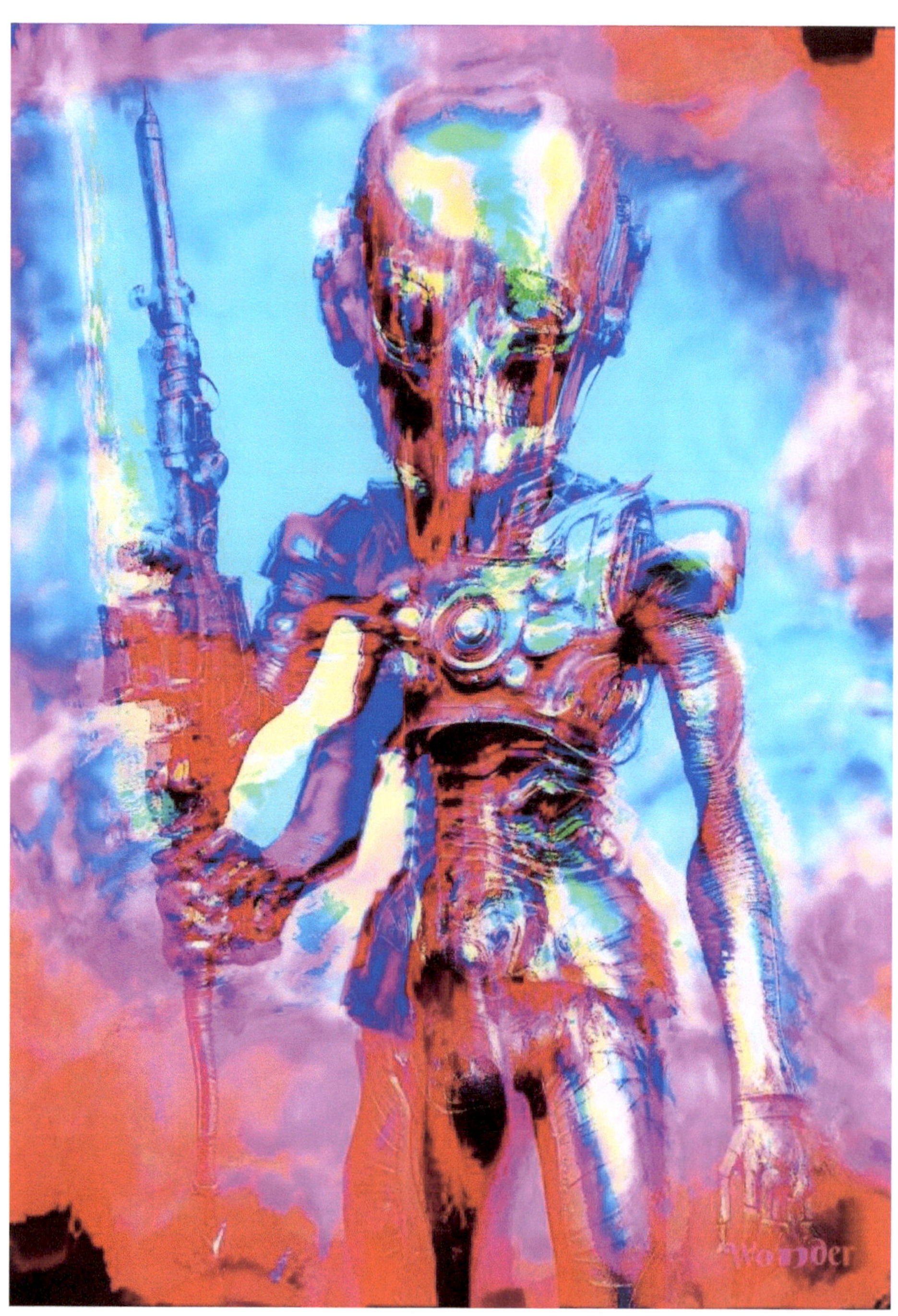

The Sadist of San Sabastian

Sanctuary, a saturated headpiece
immersed in fractured memories
delayed and calculated reactions
retracting headless and grim
a lightless dawn raging
rings once then dissolves
violently in a futile fluidity.

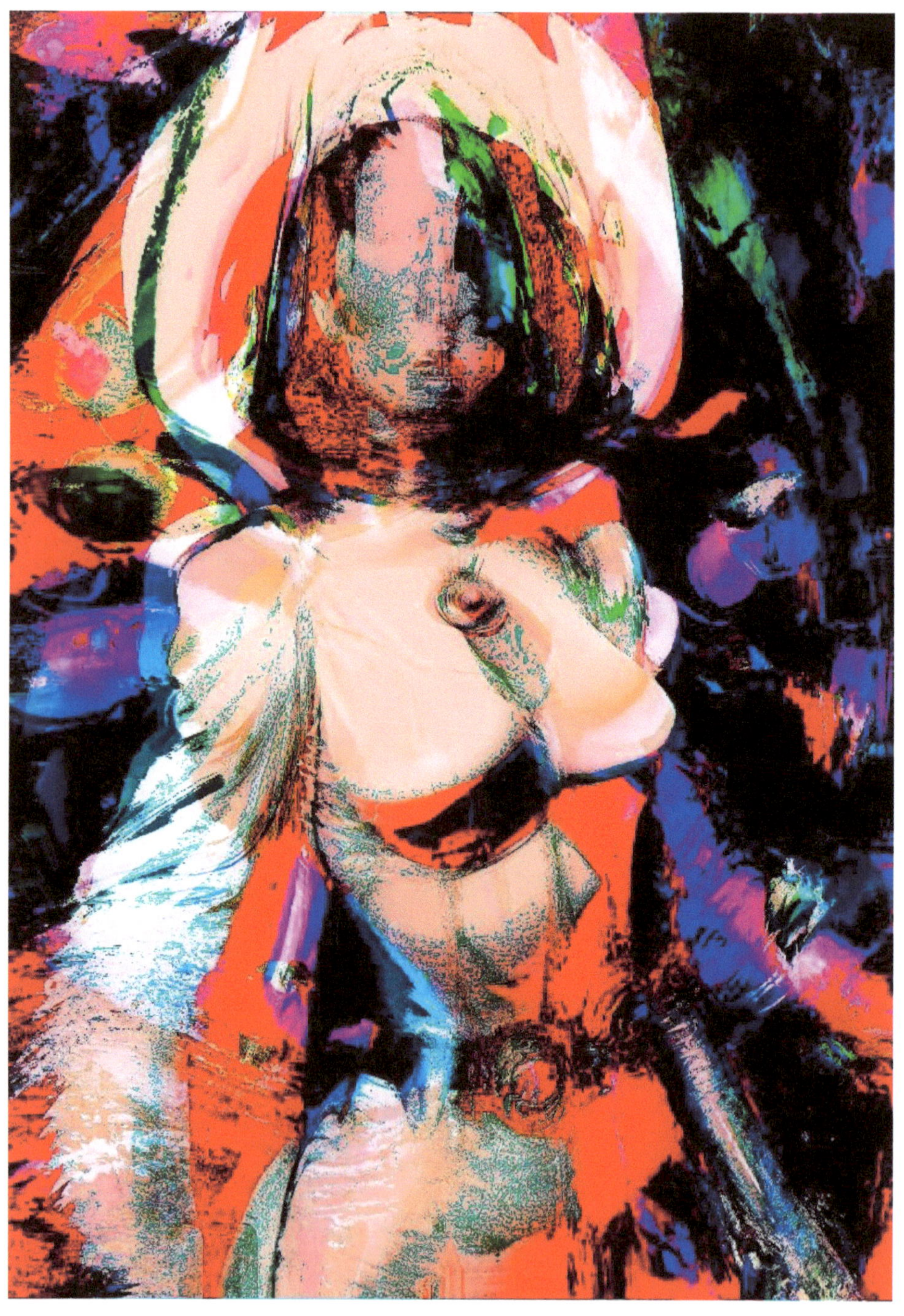

Hotter Topic Killstars

The sanctity of synchronized urination
pisshole-poor-prophets sing anonymous
without the grains that truth
we long for winters of consequence
where visions of you slaughtered dissipate
to a feral and fading future
all grounding frayed, fucked & gone
as we lose this war of language.

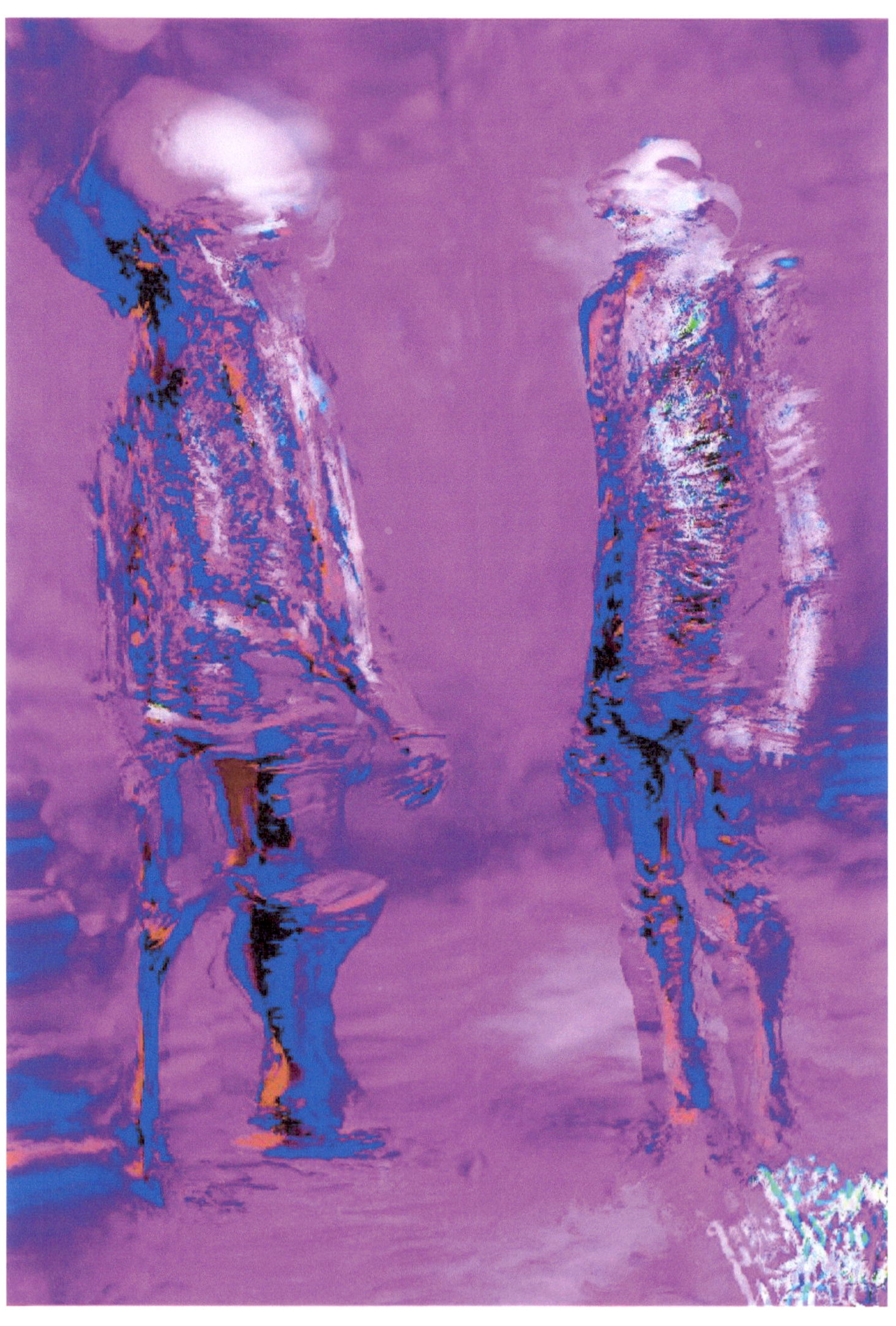

10 x Loss

My fingers are stiff from some form of physical coup
the same claimed my spine years ago
like reminders of old friends, ex-friends
reasons remain unclear
hateful and blatant brilliance
like a hunchbacked corpse
craving anal and angelic platitudes
perennial
My head, a perverse hole of sentiment
an eerily emotional excretion
shatters to the will of its brutalist desires.

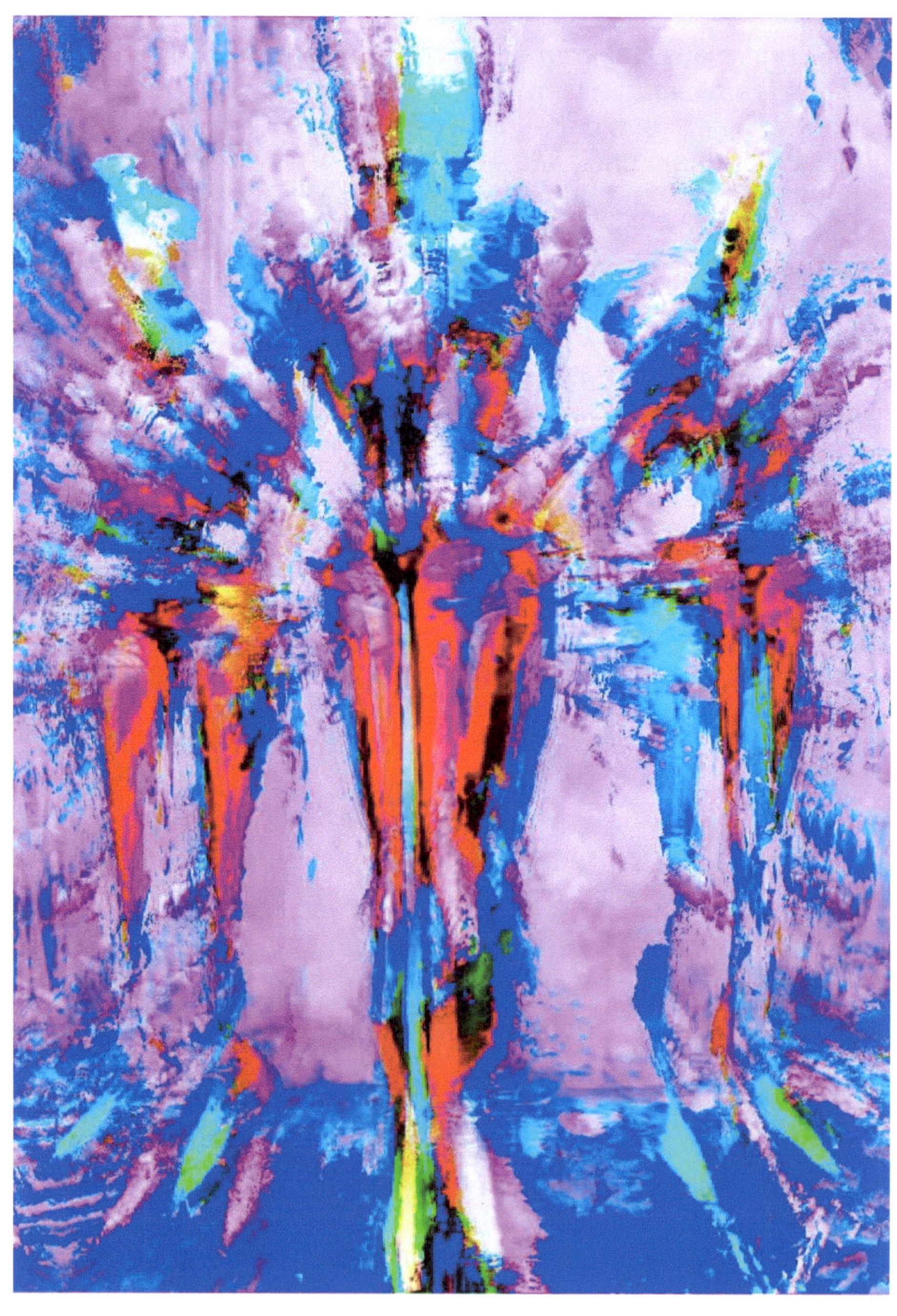

Streaming Meanies

I dreamt in dire and destruction
in whistled tones of missiles and whims
we are the genocidal voyeurs
a glorious apathy and self-annihilation
like a bow-legged goth in a field of daisies
laughing limbless
lunging lifeless
in dedication
to deification and all decapitations
the apocalyptic failure of fear
centered in hyper-sexo-sensory-severance
while we lay reckless
then wired.

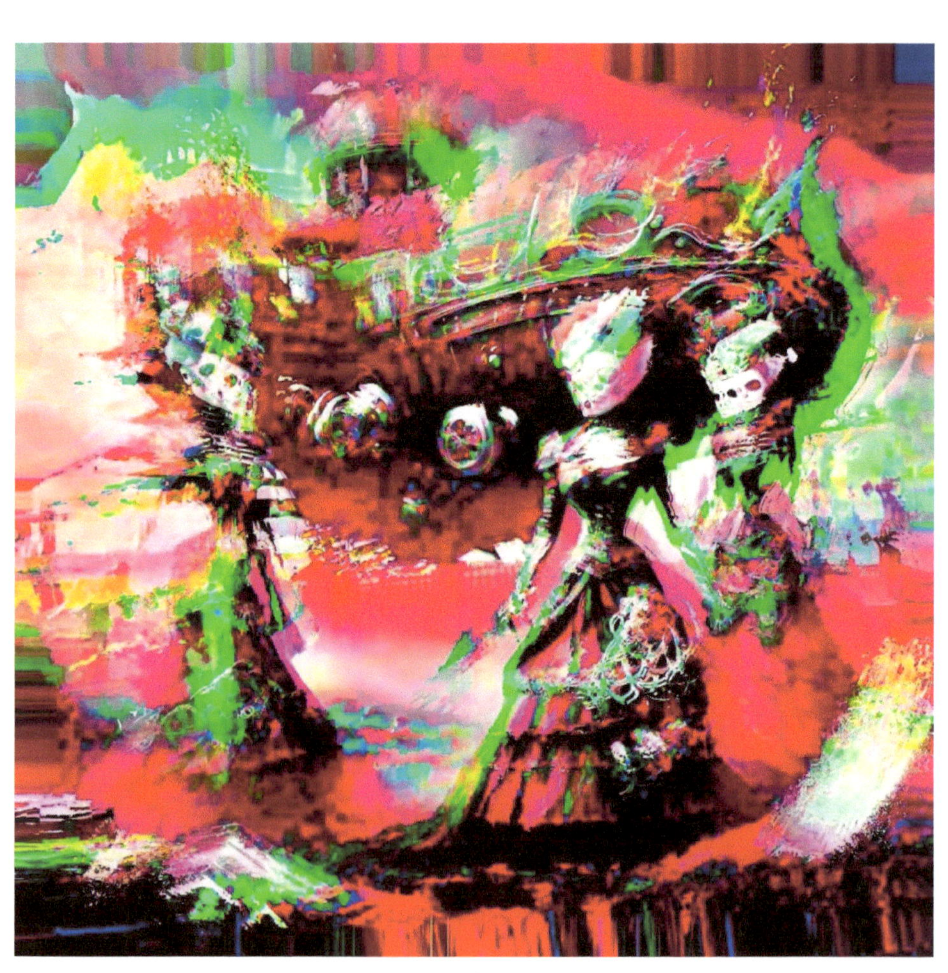

Weird, Wild, and Stillborn

Ketamine, that catharsis in white dust
like a drawn apparition quartered
a storm in swirled swelling flame
bearing witness to the angst of age
in the arms of some lewd lord
Voltaire as a contentious cunt
in vicious black veil
the trip-wires of tomorrow groan
in drop-kill-speed
THIS was thee theater of HATE
where we spoke
before violent climax.

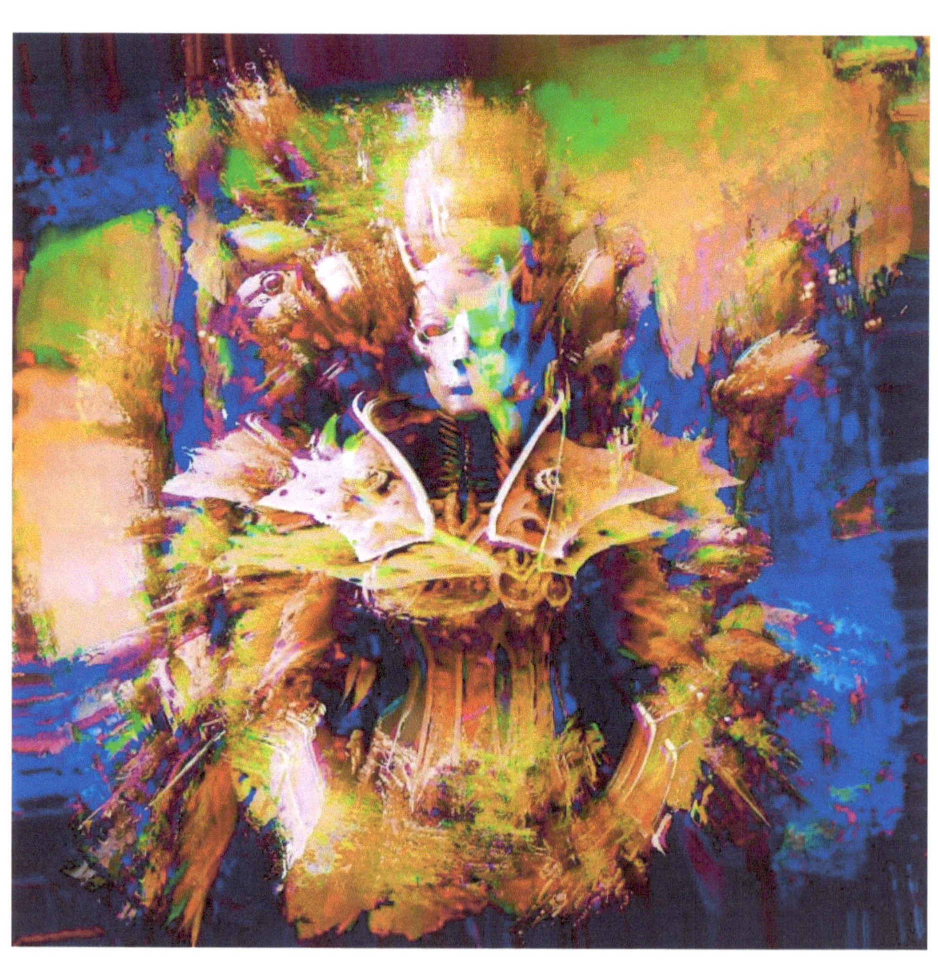

The Creepy Creeper Crept

What unclever ploy finds us windless
gutless and guilt ridden
stagnant and still
mired in mindless and mediocre
wishing I'd died in a war
....any war
16 mirrored moments of collapse
rendering inane desires mute
a self-inflicted solitude
a coven of craven creeps
relentless and potent
serving as an entrance
to that grimmest of galaxies
grieving.

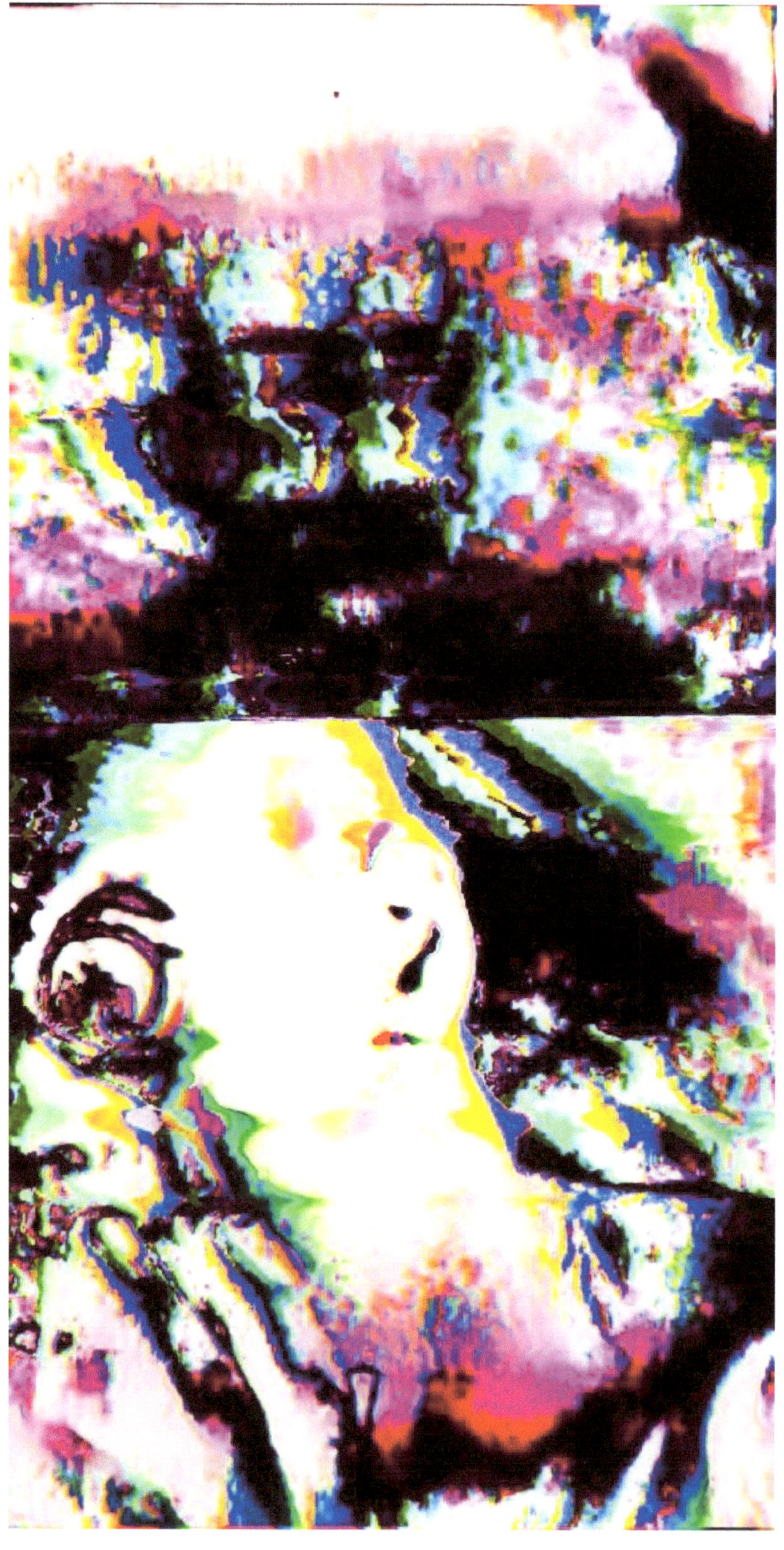

The Modulating Invaders

I am ill-prepared for anything beyond the now
daily doses of images in angst
erased moments of mental collapse
the erotic fury of sacrilegious sects
douchebags in black tees
making noise like it matters
the silence in sounds of sanctuary
pretentious and pointed
we descend joyless and broken
broken, bloody and barren
fucked off and frayed
like the voracious ending of all the things.

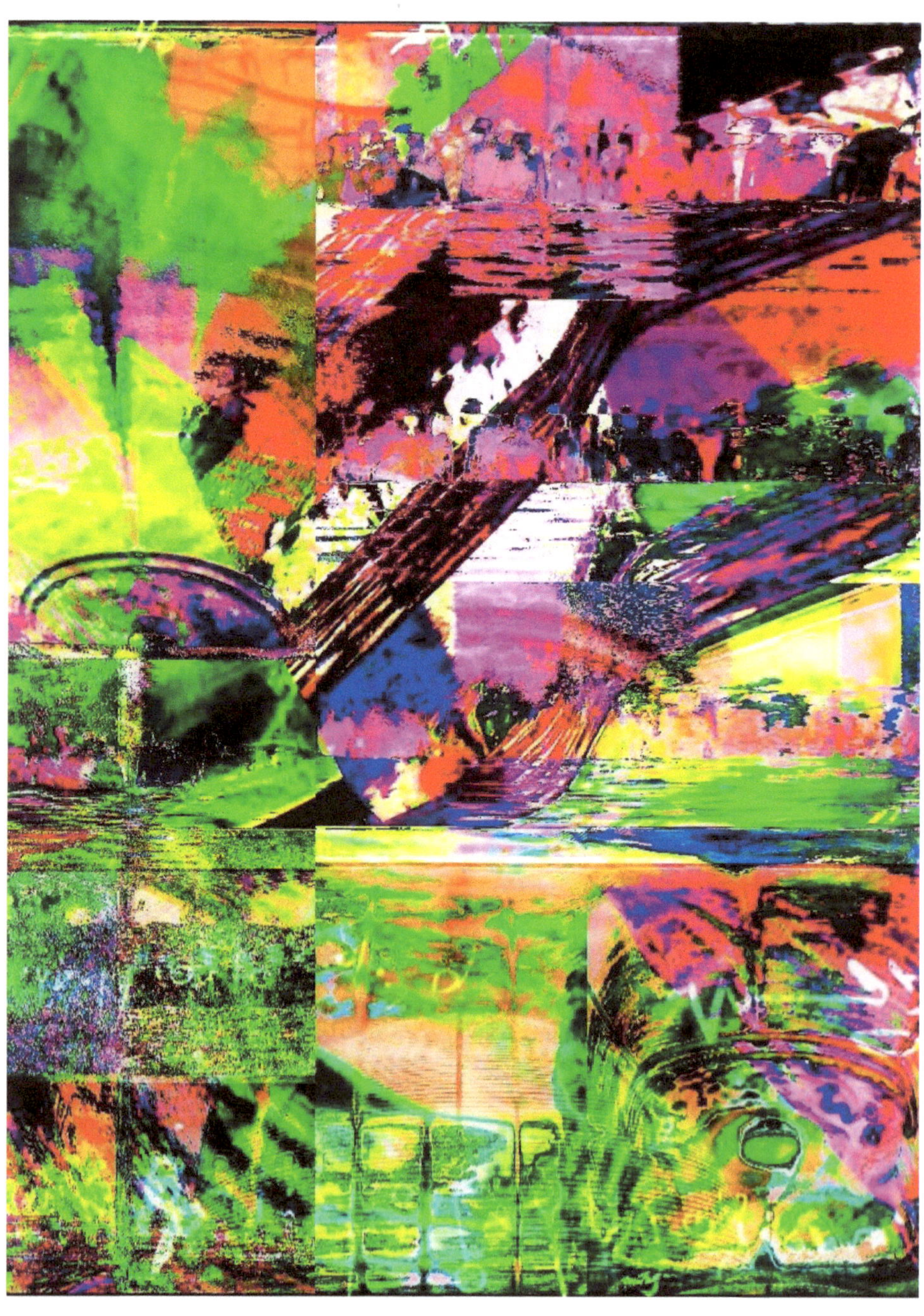

Anglo-Saxon Escape Pod

Not one thinks beyond doing
or contemplates the outsider
odd and oblivious
parentless and primitive pride
a theory of physical aboritions
your face, a longingly lit litany
of sacred and seared fantasies
sucking the life from all language
your eyes blank in the dark
never moving, never moved
a log of hundreds
etched
on two arms
numbed and toxic
in all matter of conscience.

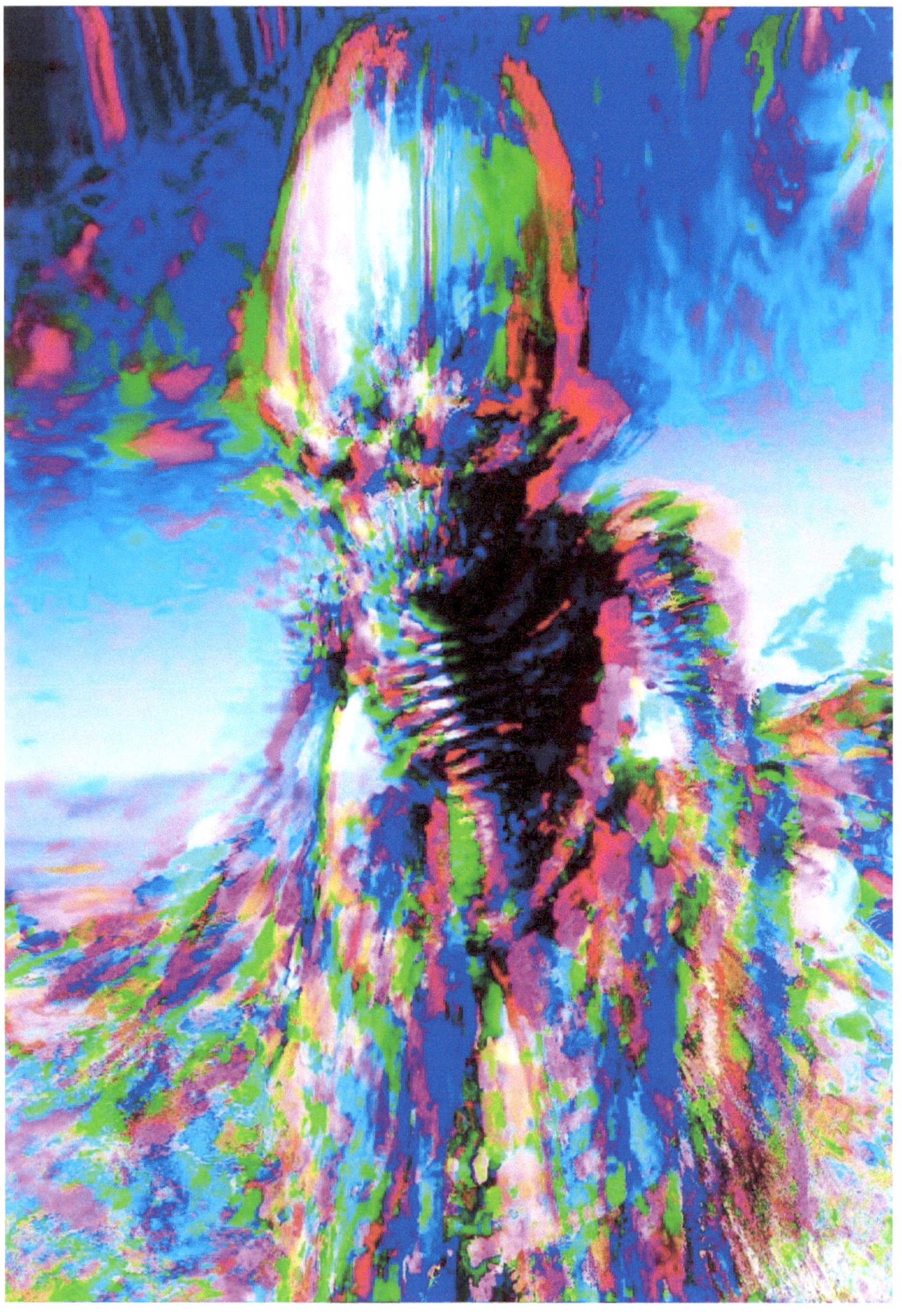

The Force of Fierce Gorapathy

Fucking migraines
methadone and moon drones
the methodology of formatted men
weapons of mass instruction
praising particles without principle
clearing a psycho's pathology
psychophantic fantasies of hell
the power of not knowing
unknowing and the unknown
a nefarian protocol
I have no message
there is no message
to soothe the unsecured
the insecure
their genocidal wet dreams
roaming lifeless and fucking reamed
in drastic denial.

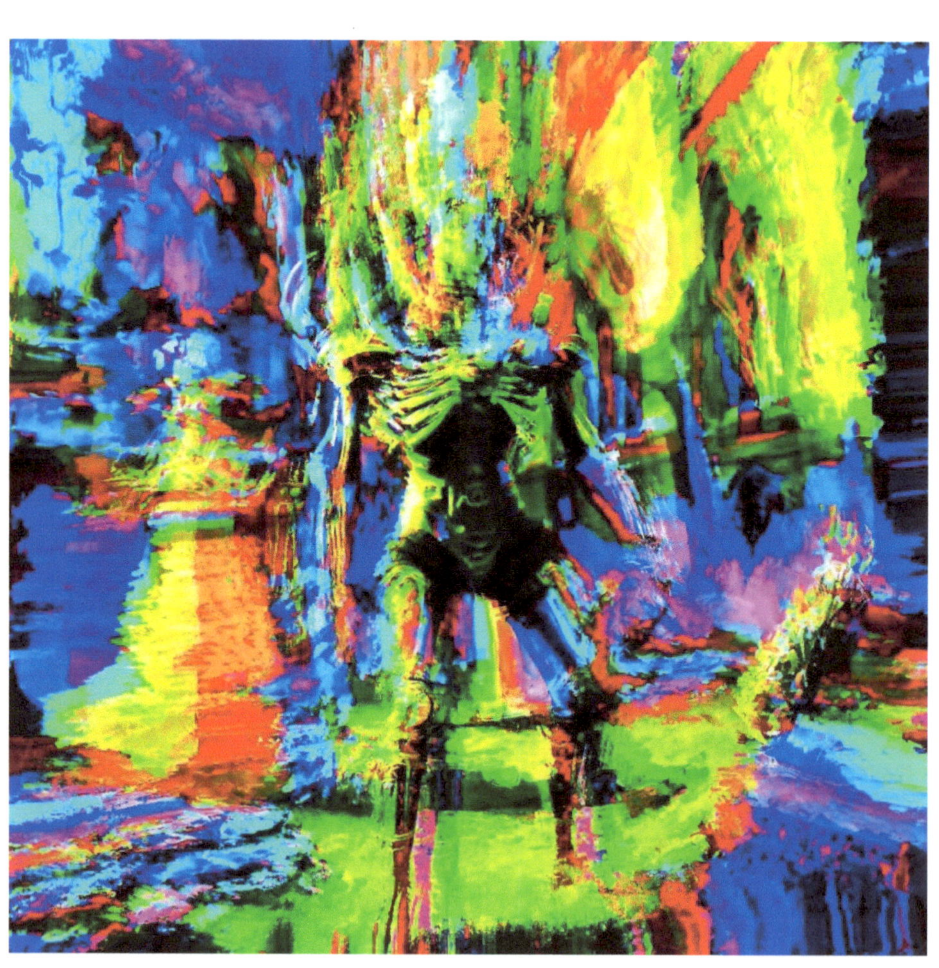

The Fucktured Nature of Forced Fears

Your words
a free-flow of misses
like cold espresso on a colder coast
4 eyes wicked and wasting
at depths of abandonment
post-doom drudgery in collapse
hands pressed seems trite
and lacking serious substance
it's a lonely room that finds me here
in a mentality of crises
confused
you reap no benefits from this
naturally.

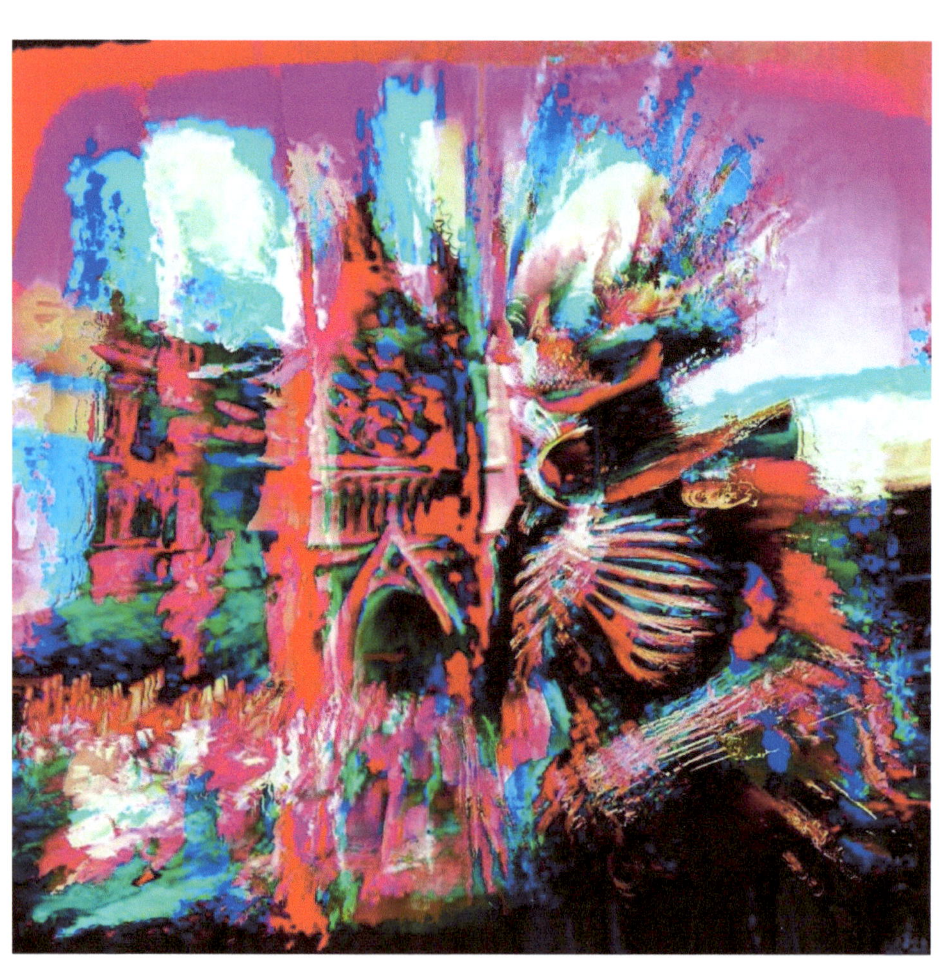

In the Midst of Mourning Everyone

Mist is that substance of self-abuse
a prism of paralyzing dream-scrapes
beyond poignant
and painful
the rocks on this coast move
when I'm not here
move when we're oblivious and sedate
we are the blind-spot we all fear
the pac-men with bottomless appetite
the missing cyber-links
...devouring space
like chocolate kisses
an epitaph worth forgetting.

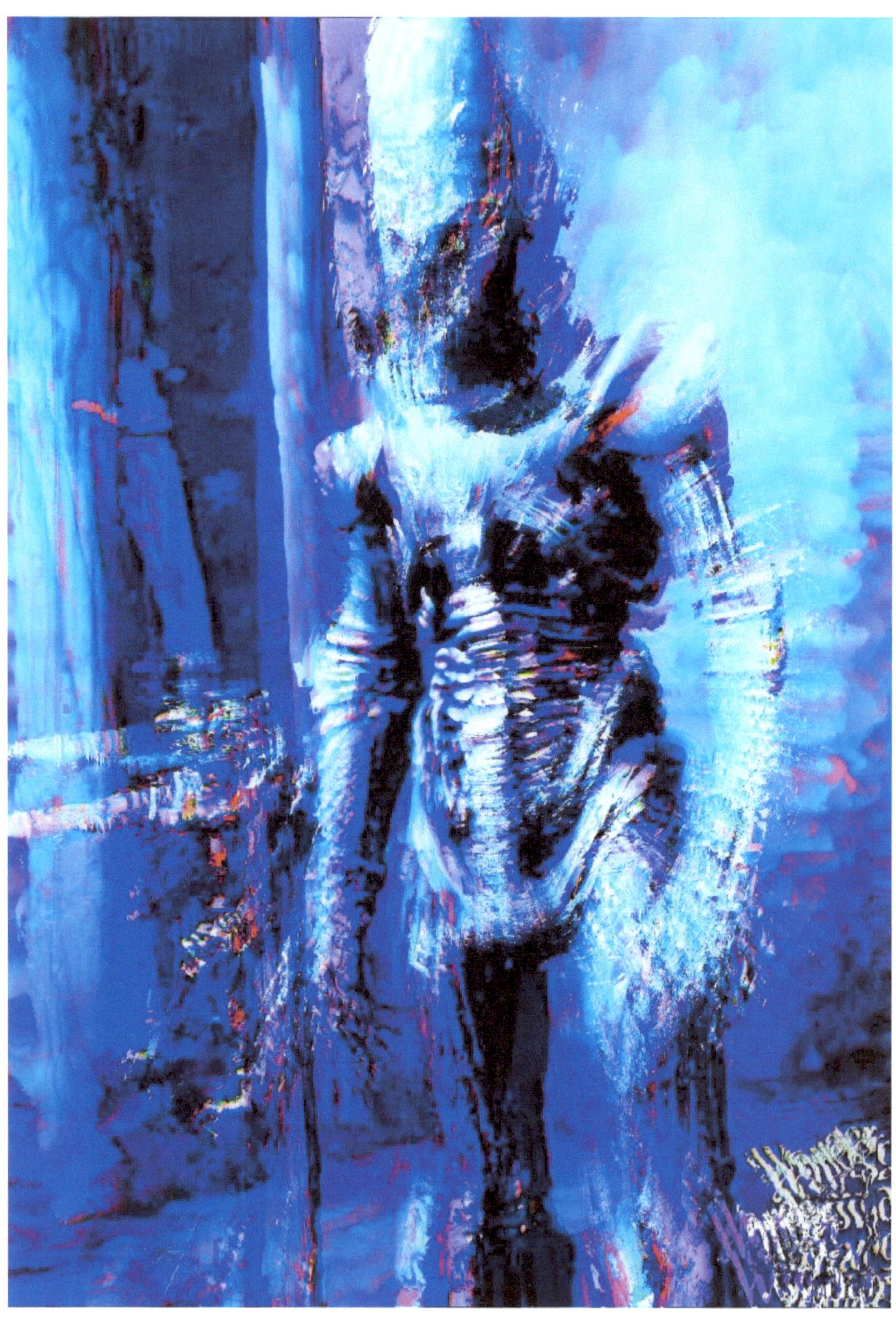

That Dreaded Source of Wonder

The house of 1000 triggers
a boy with a thorn and one arm
armed and brooding
like a nutsucking squirrel
a perpetual victim of angsty and ignorant
ranting solo nothings
in the rhythm of age
like a serial killers garden
gorgeous and gory
we are the pile that bones envy
the dreck of modern ignorance
plays then preys on all of us.

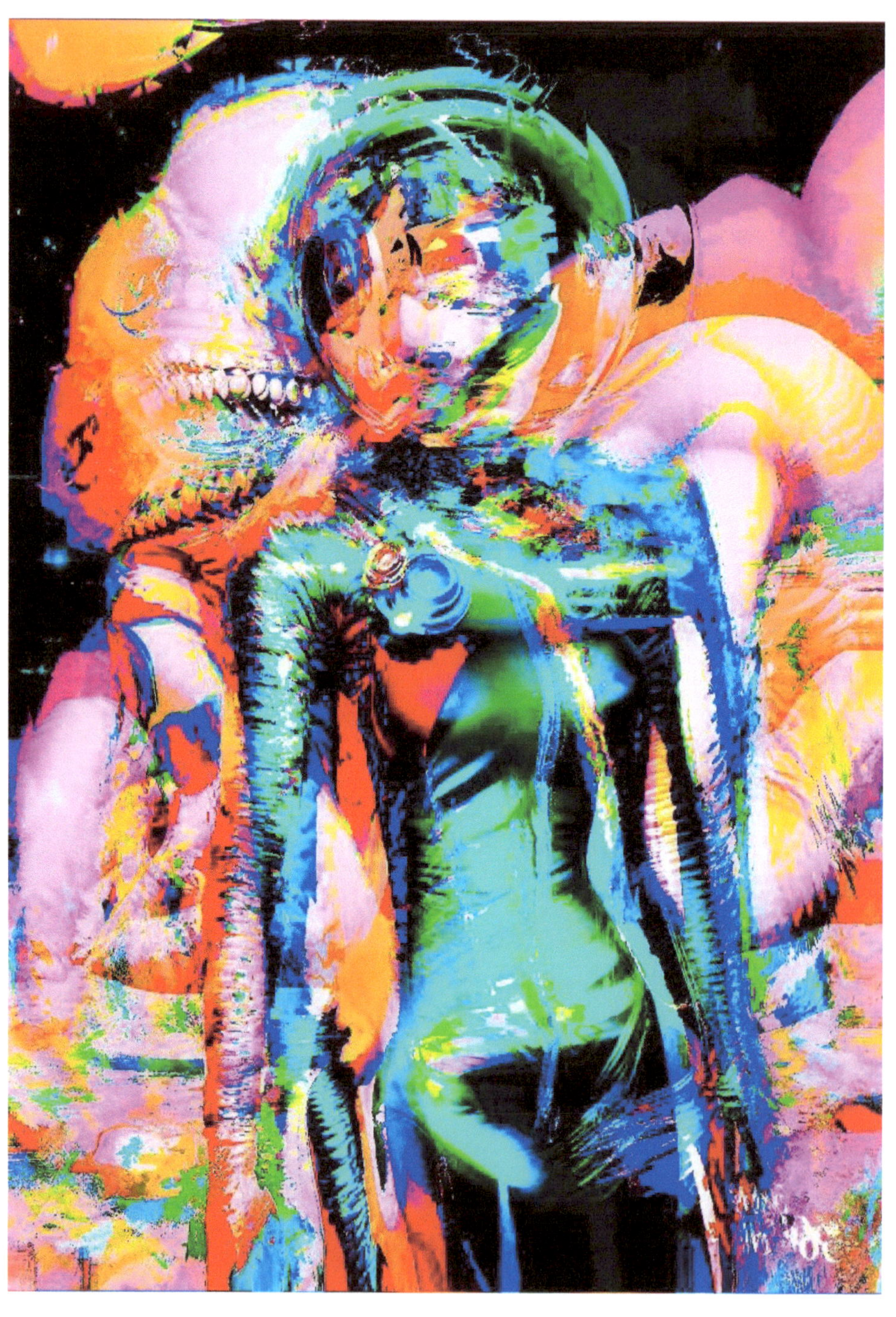

Six Sick Fucks

The end chimes are now among us
the stoic stasis of the status-quo
I am the cringer on a binge
beholding this slow demise
bound by millions
fucked by ancient fringe folklore
whilst bleeding in slowest blue
there are no promises here
no motions towards gratification
a puddle of puss on pins…
enablers for the worst in us
like a steam punked Nosferatu
identified in impartial remains
translucent and spinning
and likely to remain unforgiven.

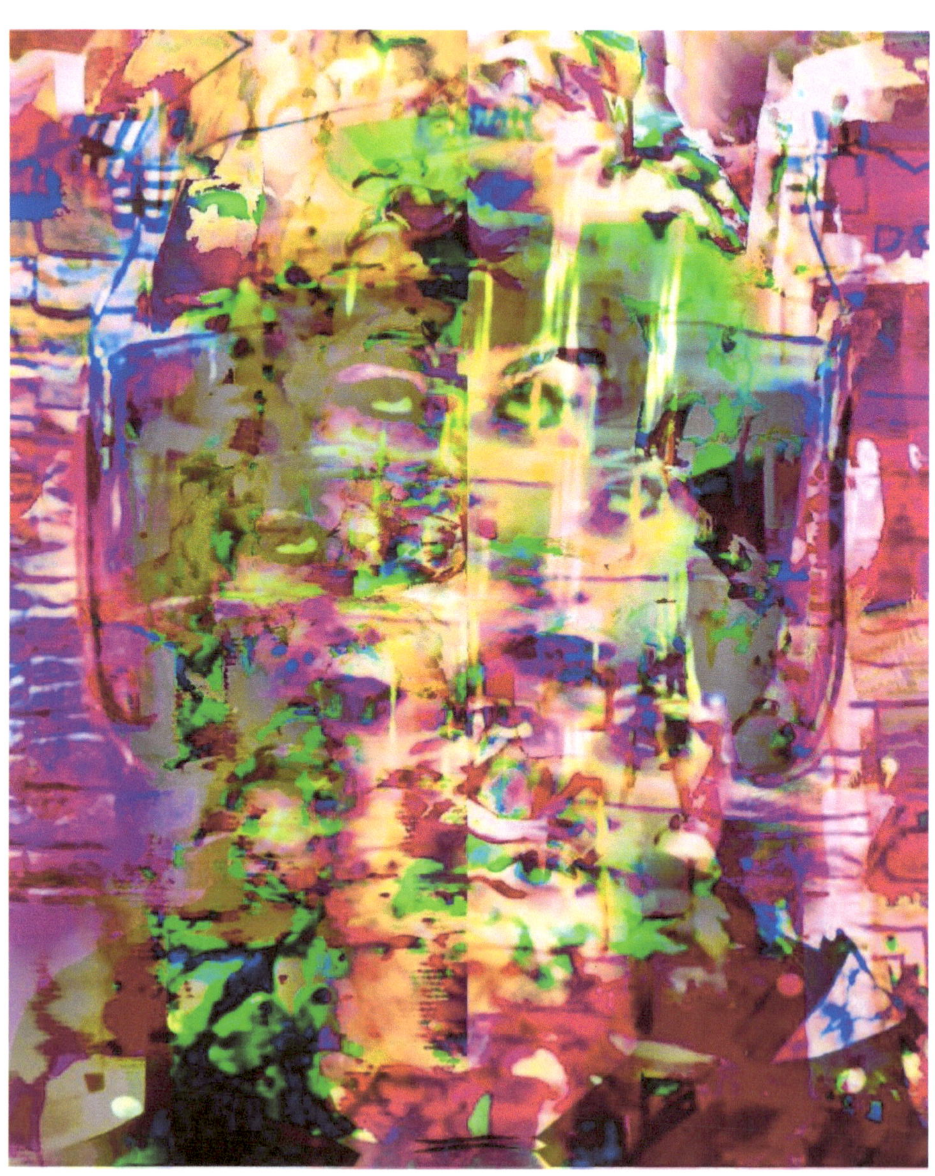

Volcanic Nature of Dissociation

Some nights bleed darker than others
blanking out vivid and at light speed
I could never spell your name with the "K" it deserved
self-served and sterile
the panic of promises
and an ill-formed grin
dreaming like a dying dragonfly
then split splintered
the spiral to an emotion ridden infinity
riding erratic and strung
to a blister graced hemorrhage.

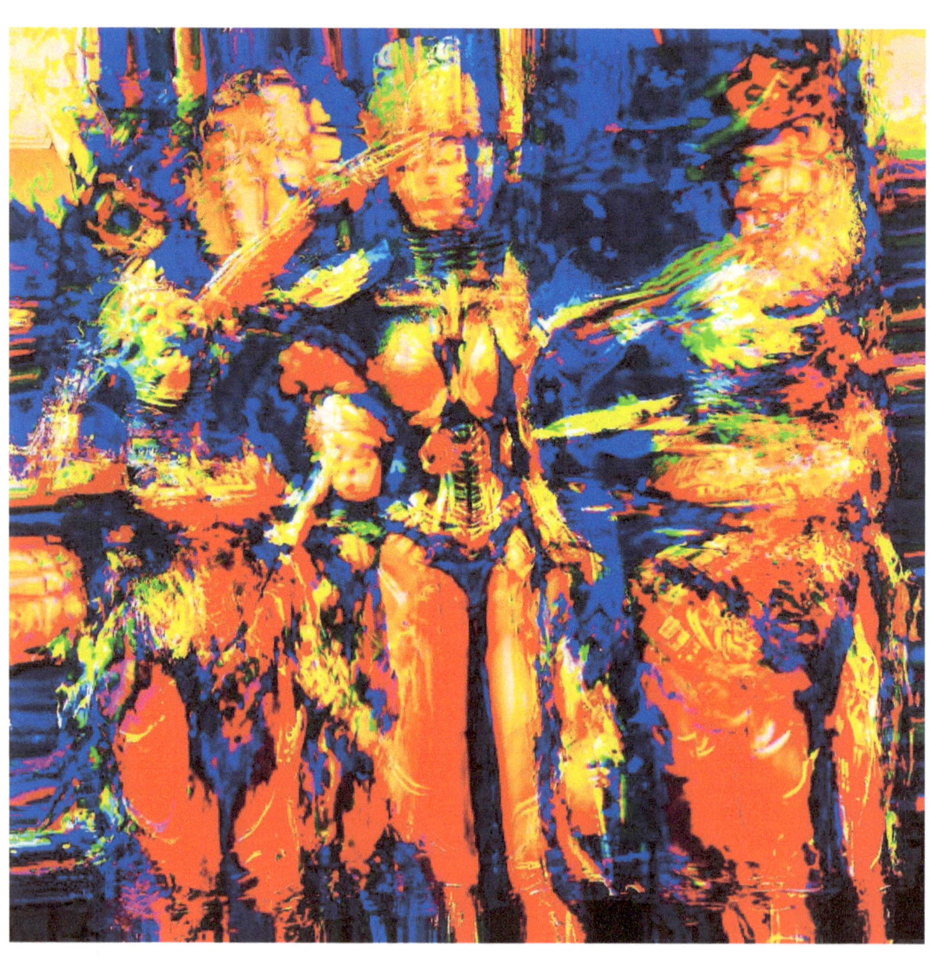

On Why it was Never Quicksand Suckers

I…eye…ī…i…aye
and the sole sucked deeper still
the permanence of unwelcome change
sucked to even deeper depths
do you deflate at a certain hour?
like an anthem for the maladjusted
swinging
like hangry testicles in molten winds
a fierce cultural swing
porn addicts ascending
in the preferred context
soaked then suckered into primal pretense
nutsucking “civil warriors” cry sickly
then surrender
in the face of the deceiver
and a well balanced blasphemy.

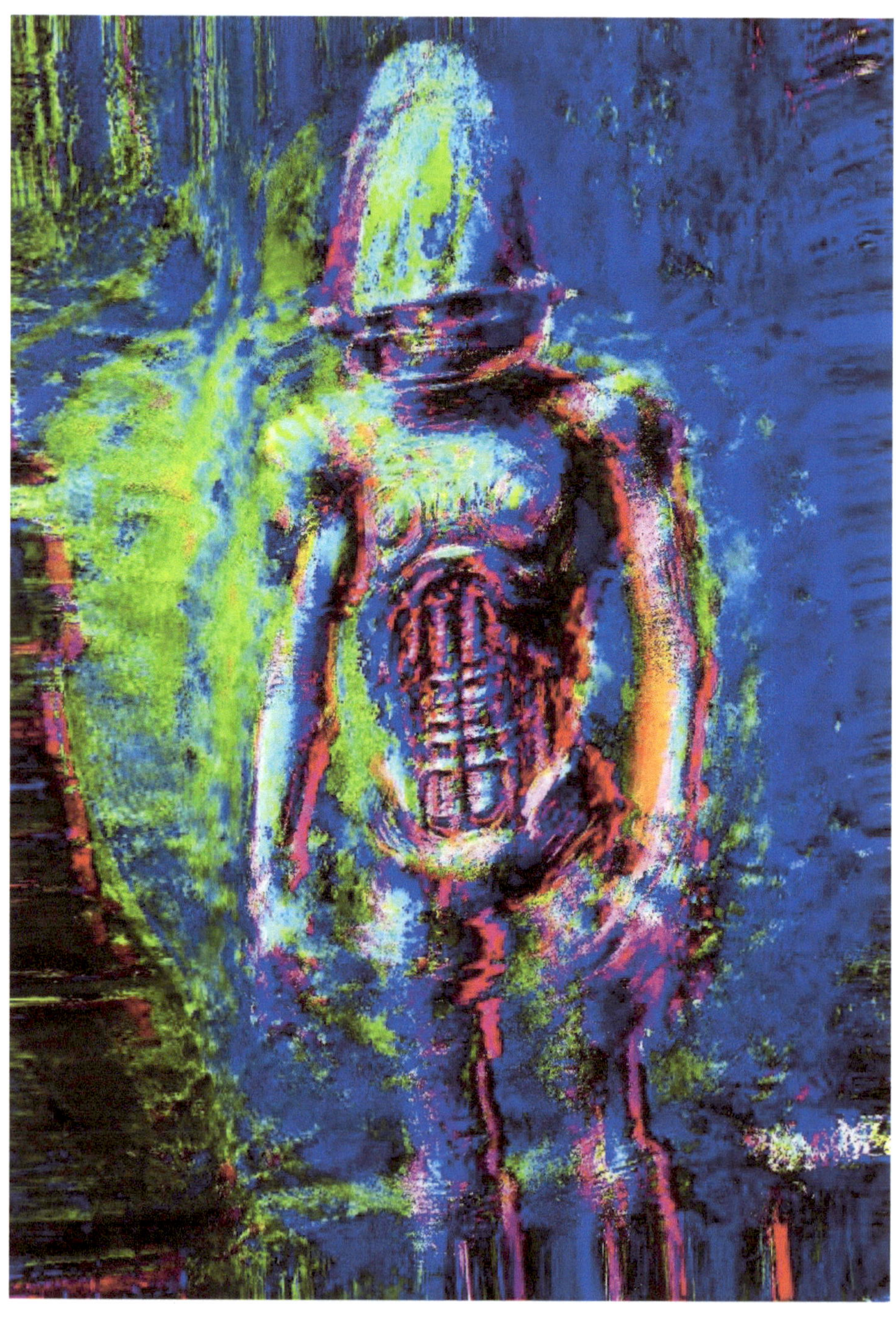

This Rotting and Regressive Reich

This planet will eradicate you…us
in a haze of violent glory
cited in modulating black noise
distant crawlers and crumbling
there was never a way out ya know
a barrage of too soon
three slumbering sirens
signal lost cause
then collide
on mechanical mountains
abrasive and beautiful
beyond the sacrifice
and suffer.

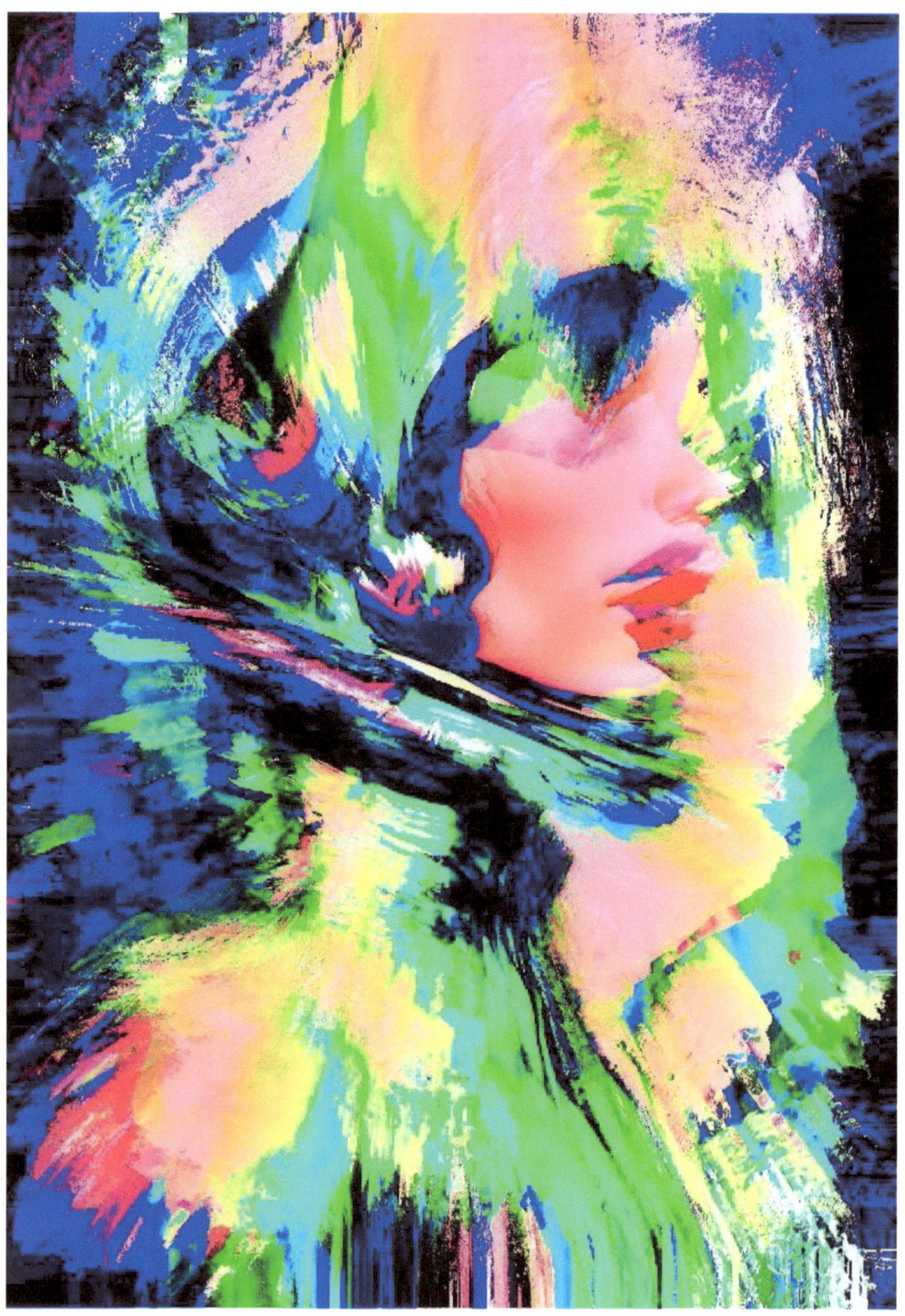

That Inevitable Wave of Horror & Guilt

Those fangs you built no longer pierce
...nor puncture
a pure and perilous misconception
hurricanically stoic
your largest birds float like air
suffocating
godlike hands strangling
a kitten climbs heavenly
clutching for horrific reprieve
hidden
in an android of arms
the complex ignorance in all things
striped...stripped...serrated
then burned ‘til benign.

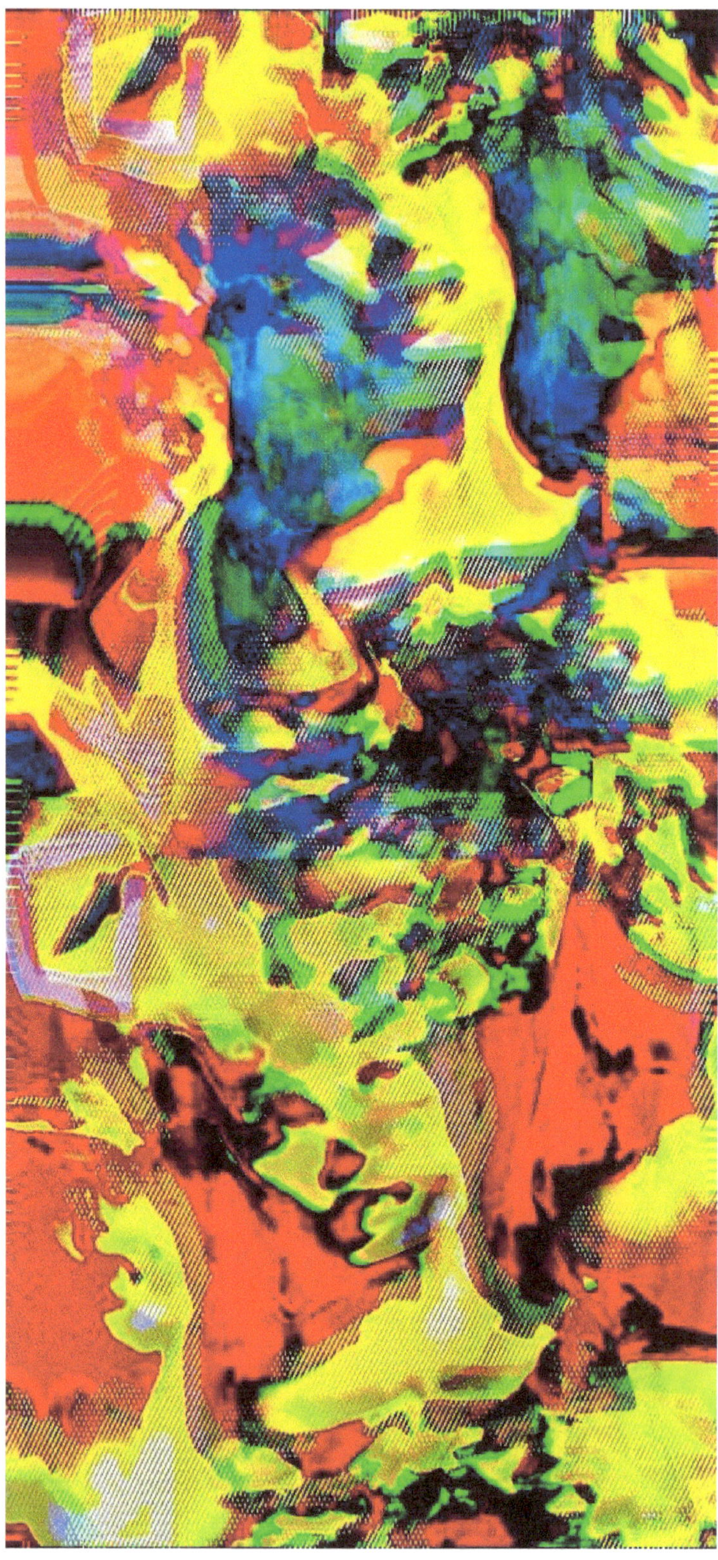

Serial Submission and the Economy of Loss

Loss is the length of all spaces
in rancid yet radiant spasms
spasms of chaotic synchronization
we are the dissident distractors
inducing crass and fascist wet-dream
the totality of tongues clashing
from frail to volcanic raging
you're the hose held to hot waters
the predetermined parasitical prey
the harsh pounding of a coerced grim
circuits of brilliance banished to ash
folded like raw skin and dried
that weird flex to a hostile trinket
to the implosion of all that matter.

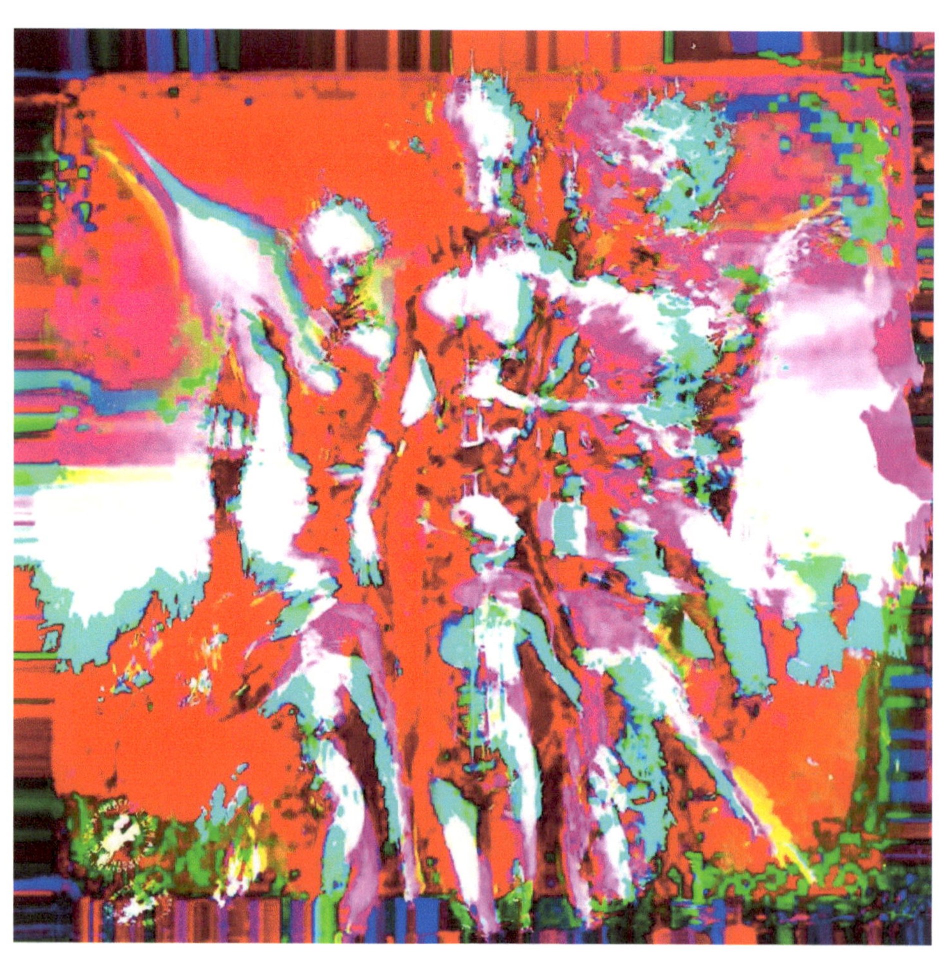

The Critical Cortex of ZERO Context

A landscape draped in hatred
the Xtermination of the silent and the sane
in a loop of deep and millennial moments
the fucked up origin of all skeletons
the blood soaked gutz of a gruesome Gotham
your deity is a bloviated shit-sack
preying on false premise
you glide on past slopes til senseless
sleeping in the sand of a billion worms
Ave Maria Ave Maria
an ode to a joyless destruction
deemed depraved and derelict
in this holiest of hell storms.
XXX XXX XXX XXXXXX

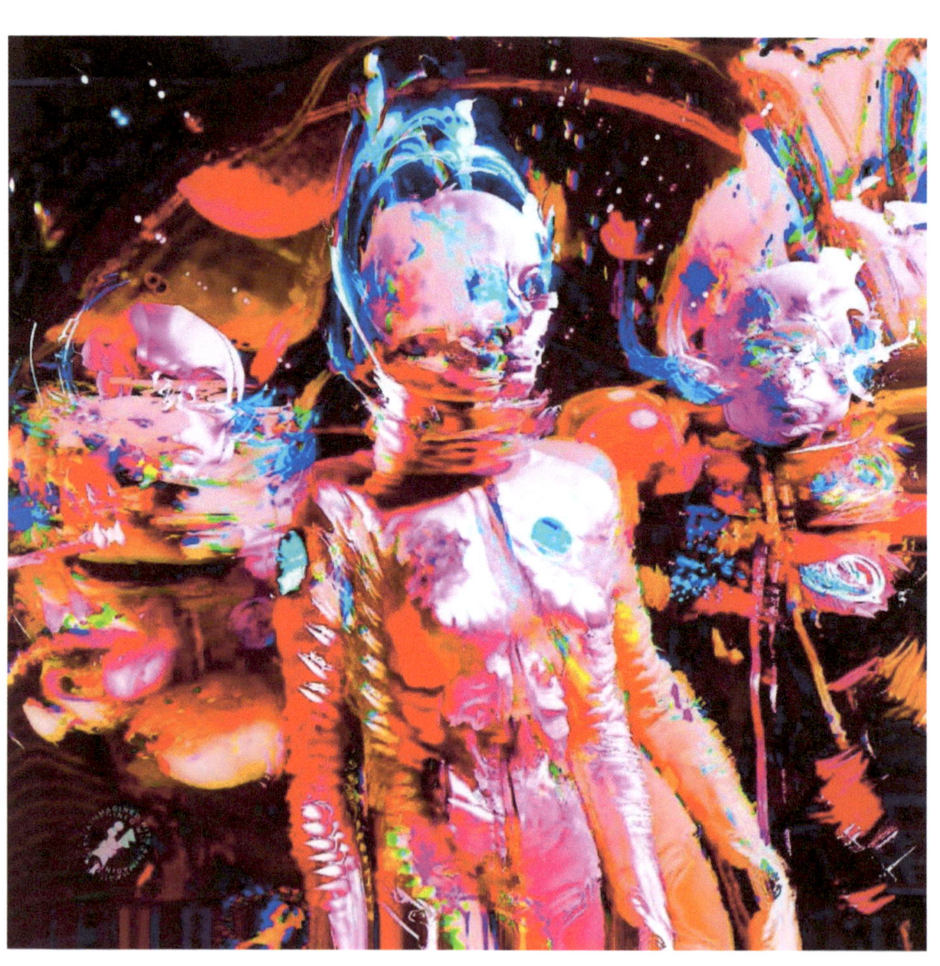

The Seriousness of Anti-Matters

Pretend and pretentious scenarios
locked in a cultural stop-motion
the annexation of bent and bitter brains
on knights of broken glass
palms to our heads collectively
a sinking and insecure sanity
the blank art of conforming
a legless cycle of spinning
the spineless
in a bay of spears
the stigma of stagnation pounds
as a cult rages relentless
death as an article of expression
the convention of extermination
speaks at heinous volumes
I am THEE prophet
the singular & self-proclaimed nothing.

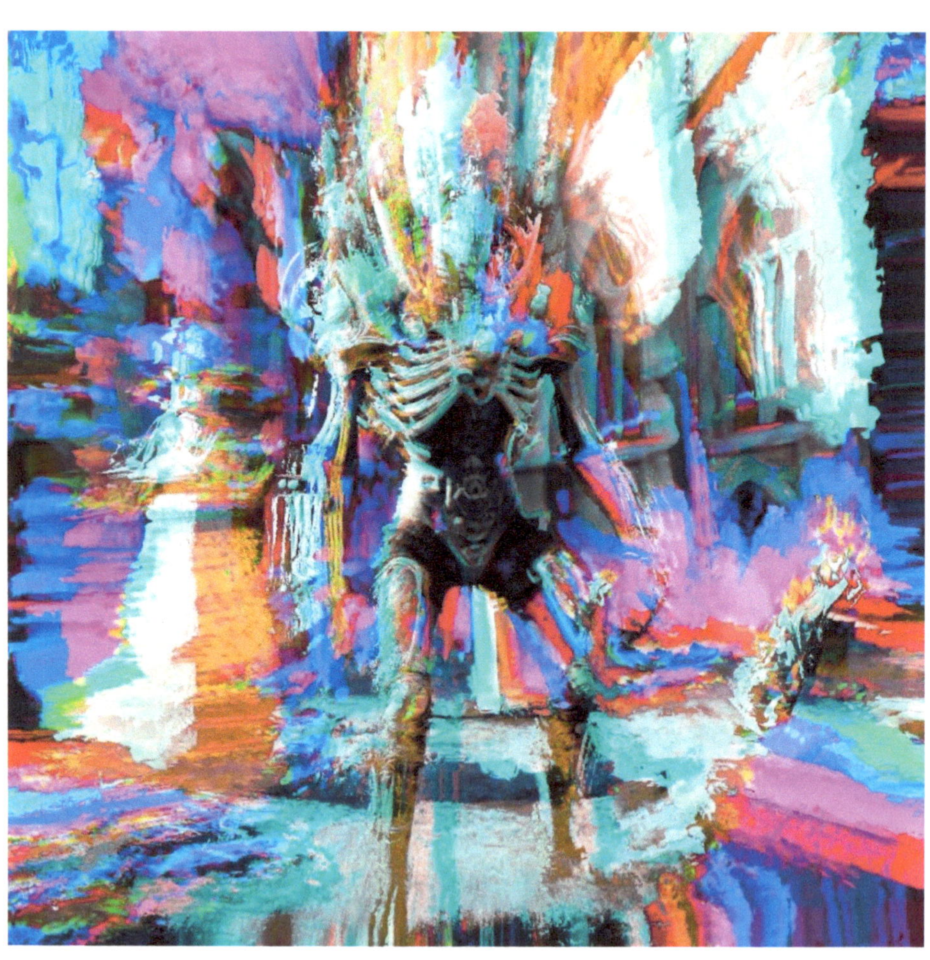

The Draining Dirge of a Death Machine

Backwards we march
mercy-free
malicious & murderers
the sting of bold truths
on the liars that breed them
blatant beatings to bloody
they're fucked
…we're fucked
always fucked
forever fucked
cherry-picked and unprincipled
here is where the body ends
replies cease or never
a deranged circus pounding
pummeling shoddy retreats
stingers
from known assailants sting
and keep stinging
the mass grave of empathy
and the apathetic morpheme
placing sticks on amplified stone
crossing over
to aery ZERO.

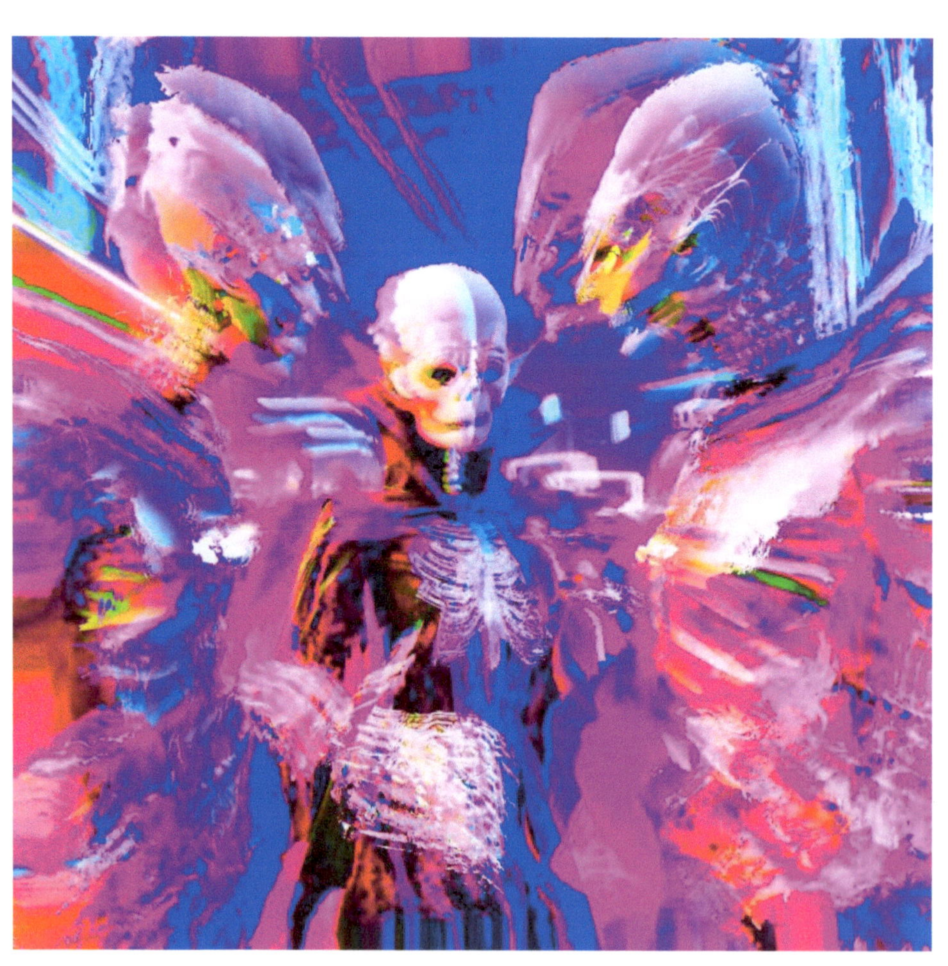

Subversive Practices w/ Concrete Repulsions

Your rhymes are an abysmal illusion
a repulsive tone mainlined
every moment marking death
drawn to primal timings
incoherent ramblings
I miss everything
I still miss everything
I still miss everything about you
without remorse
like a vicious and giant spider
or an enormous shark preying
we'd watch for hours
insatiable and salient
somehow
like lifetimes ago
dreams that woke the dead
wake destructive desire
with no distance cited
the trick here being HELL
but nearer
nausea
that'd make that gargoyle gag
on a diet of self-destruction
derailed and determined
for the banal & beauty beyond.

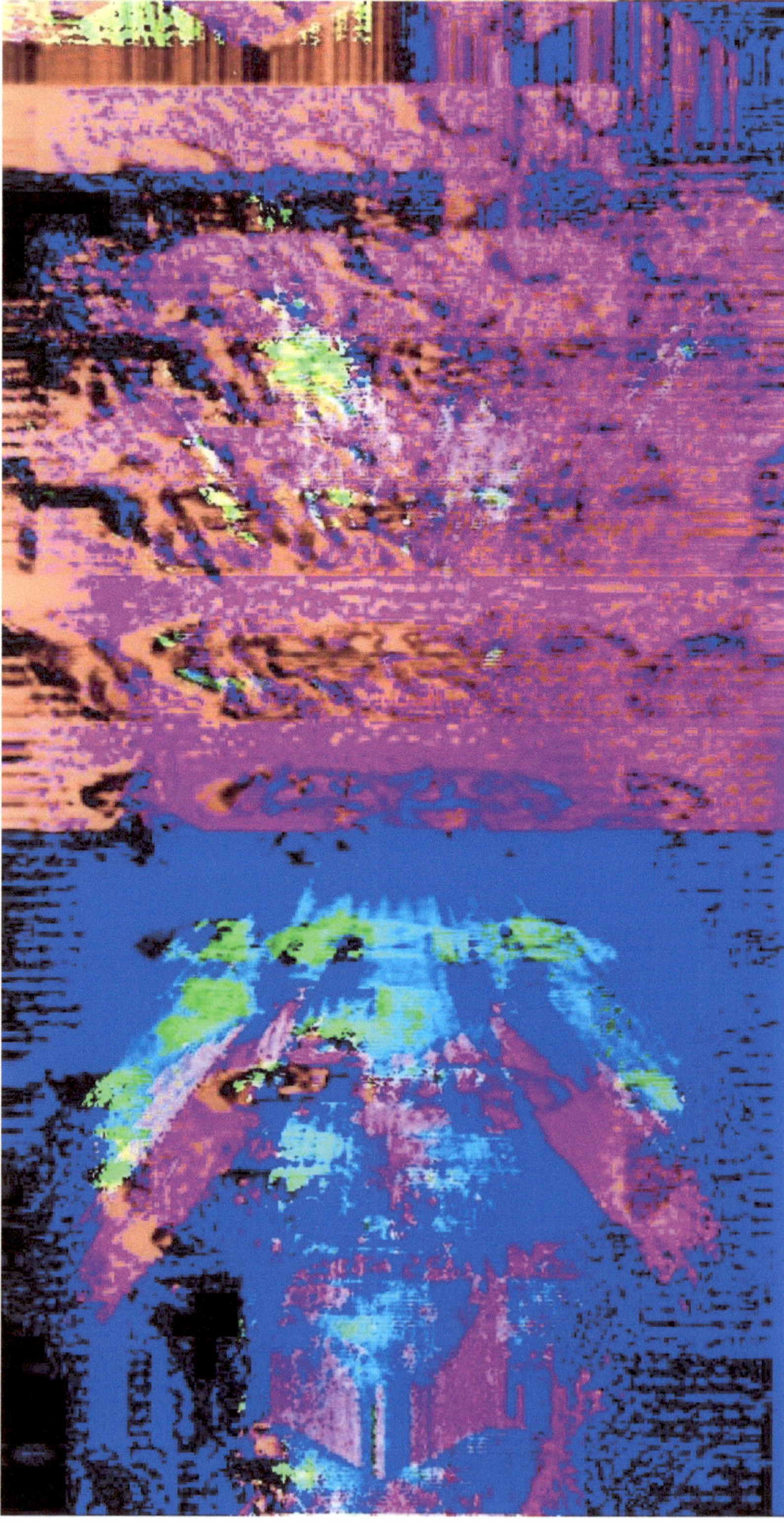

A Safe-Place at a Predators Pace

Everyone is sooo fucking whacked out
strung on years of wild stupid
conspiracy driven fuckwits
diving
deriving pleasure from the pained
pinned to an abominations call
all of it a calculated scheme
mutating and subhuman
your past pitiful as you are pale
we are the products of others WE ARE
warped, broken and inbred
a horror film with the saddest end
these symptoms of disbelief
systems piled on systems bleeding us bound
and brooding
a black box buried
in a white room
whilst yelling FUCK IT BLUE
in a solid mass with no mercy
I'm done. Done.

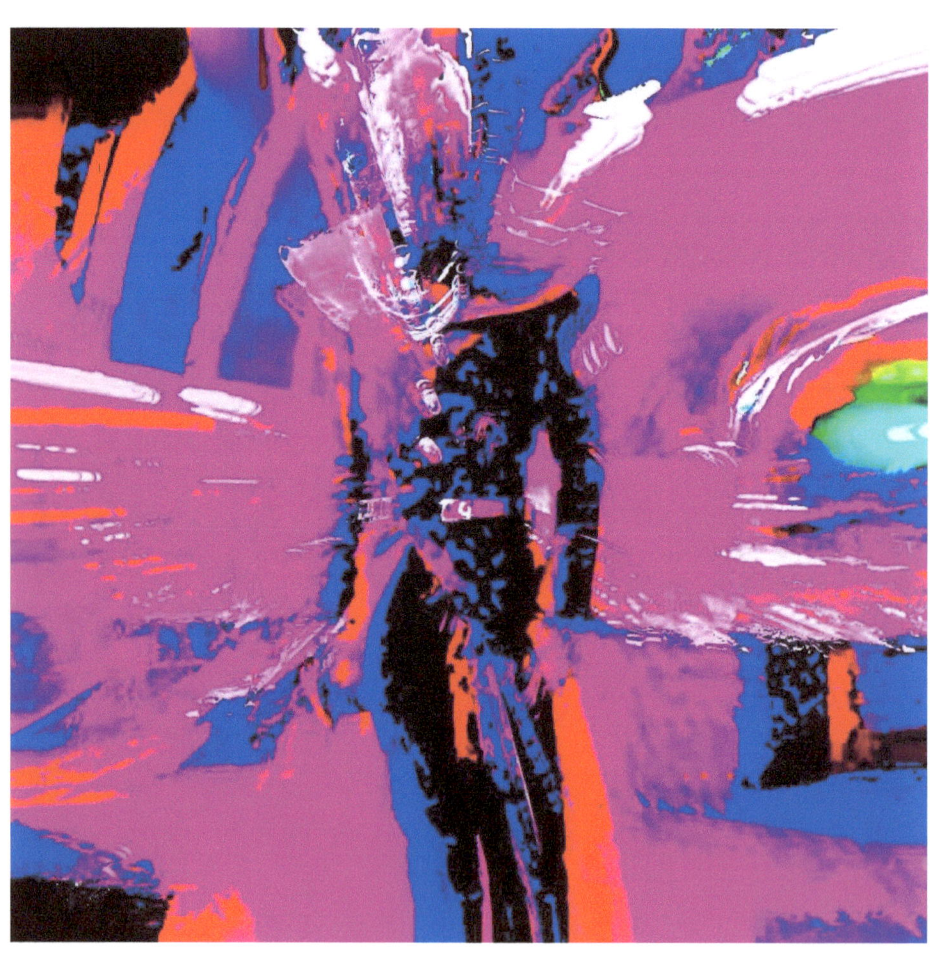

Sin and Your Viretic Exo-Skeleton

These dreams are fucking brutal
bitter and biting doom collages
a plague of imagery
equal to
your aversion
to psycho-sexual evolution
that poorly written psalm
a putrid corpse with a handy cock
never to be read out loud
a religion of doom-scrollers
provide dystopian dramas
both pummeling and promise
I'm tired today
and THAT is where these thoughts end.

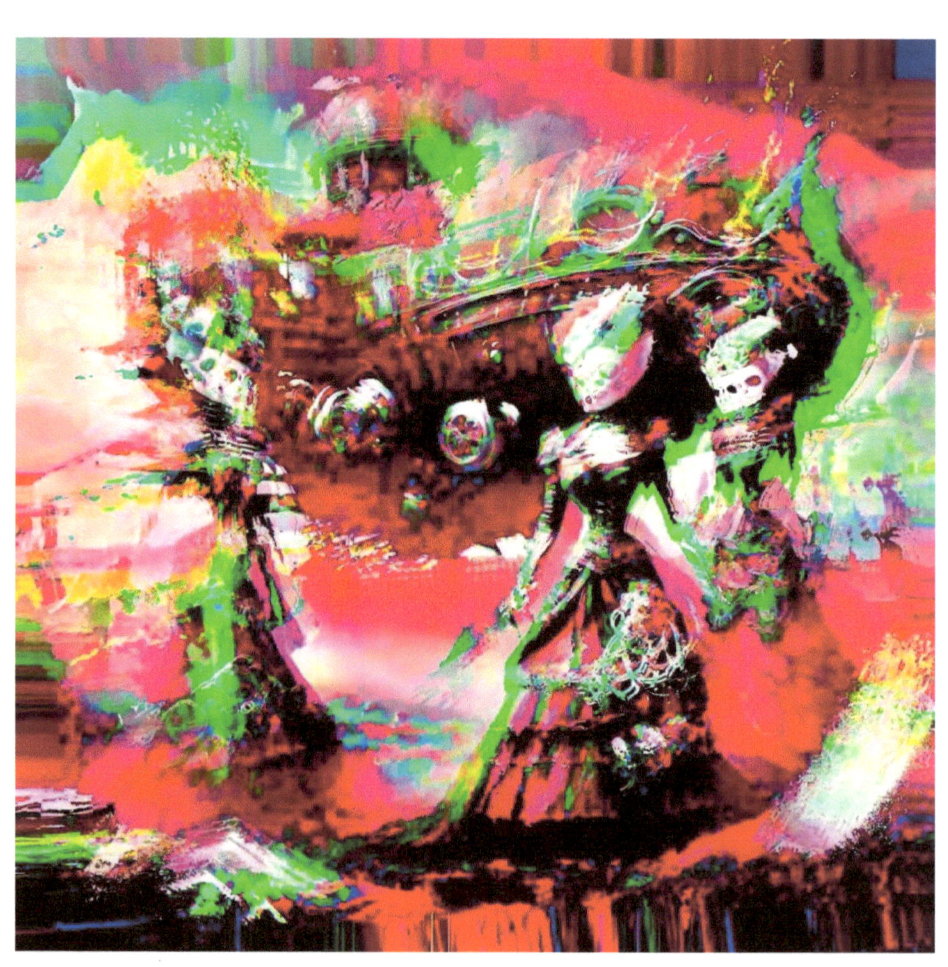

All of This Pain, I Assume I'm Dying

Noise is an irresponsible moment
an impossible passage of time and more time
like disintegrating in slow motion
disengaged and driving
what feels like forever
over and over and over again
the year that stood still
still
reliving that fucking moment daily
hourly, minute by minute
a singular sorrow
I saw it…did nothing
a pitifully frail failure
in lapsed liquidity
I'm never fucking high enough
never fucking high enough
fucking never
a sanctimonious shitstorm
reverting to a slowwww crawl
for another damn year.

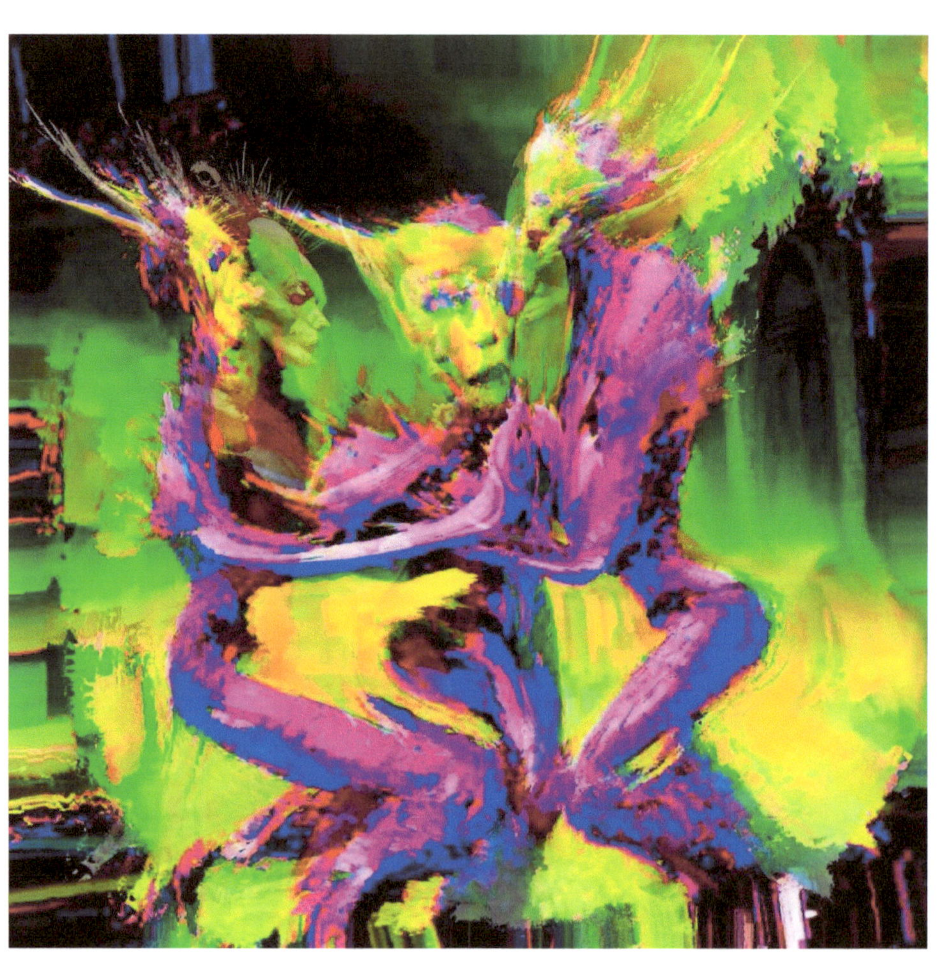

I am the Museum for Random and Rancid Bullshit

The inevitability of collapse
the sounds of a thousand sirens buzzing
It'll be sad when this invasion ends
like everything really
exhaustion is a failed language
at this point
numb and numbing
a forced spiritual biopsy
and braindead
a funnel of the misinformed
forming and foaming mouths
the ignorance of the bored and boring
tongue to pole
pronounced terminally treading
directionless words are unused
the pitfall of the petulant and the pious
an autopsy on the subconscious
as we reign in the remains
placed on unrepentant repeat
then
in a fever of psycho-fucking-matic
we repeat it once again.

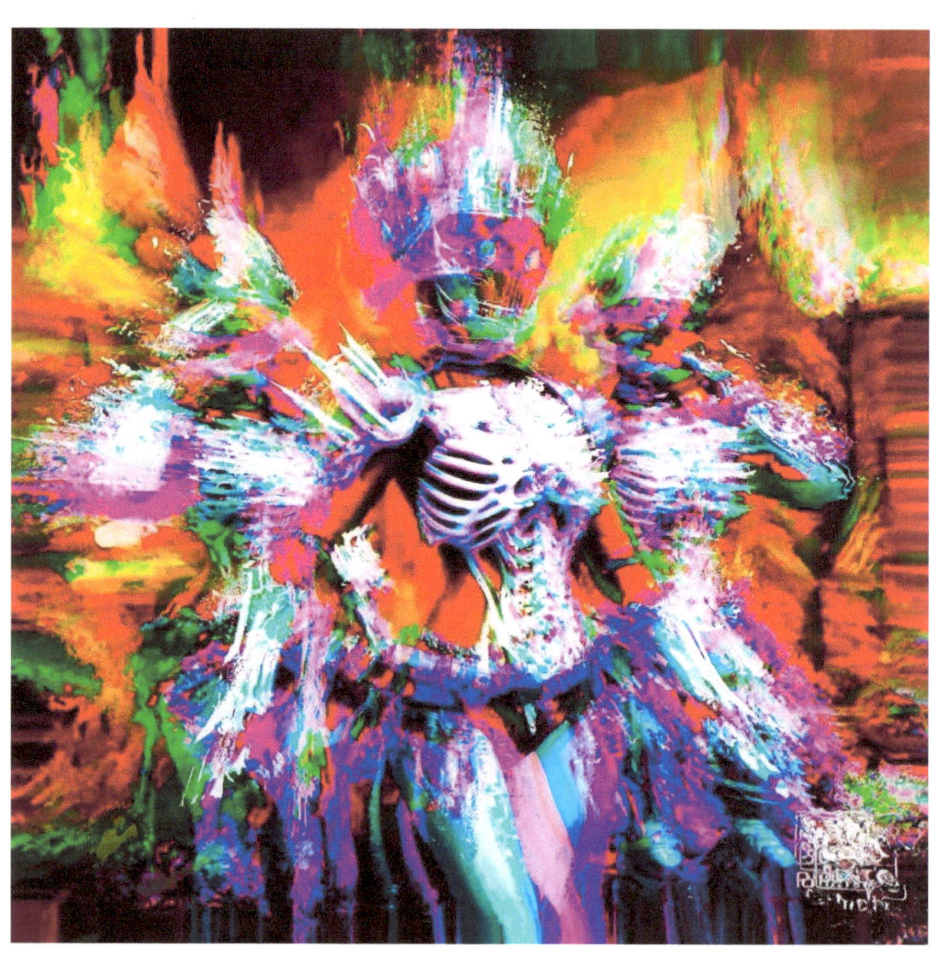

Dreaming in Death's Drones

"Artists" are the earth's asshole
on a loop spun in banalities
spun on pretentious reflection
a rabid teddy bear and a lost cause
a gruesomely carved torso
with christ-like posture
dialed up and depraved
it is all so fucking impossible
the self-inflicted nocturnal beatings
ramped up ramblings of the brain severed
time passing in a loop of errors
stirring universal ill-will
struck…molded…then displayed.

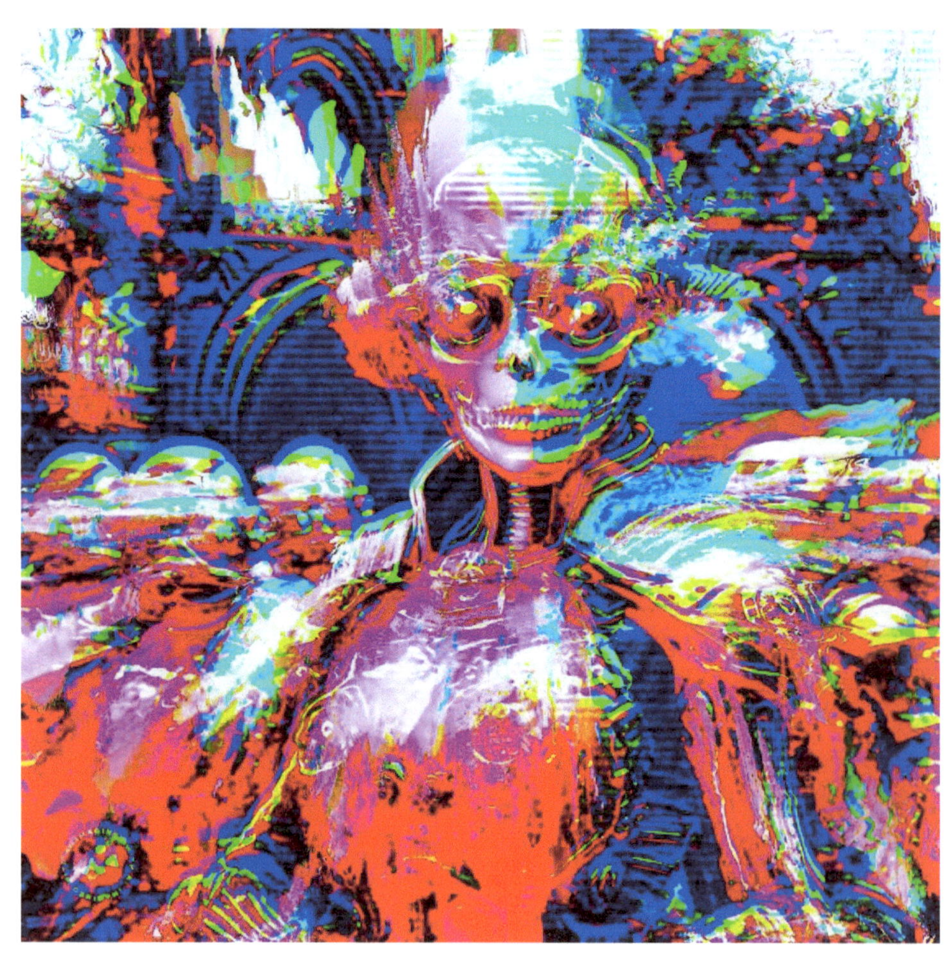

A Cave Dweller's Anthem

Every day more beauty leaves
this space to that dead place
a suspension of total collapse
all barriers now broken
mocking cult-juiced fuckjobs
breaking
from a pack of monolithic and murky
a fixer with futures fucked
a sublime lack of understanding
drowning in coerced gesture
as viewed through the mania of monochrome
perfectly released then recycled
I drove there alone for that reason
all are parts of my beautiful decay.

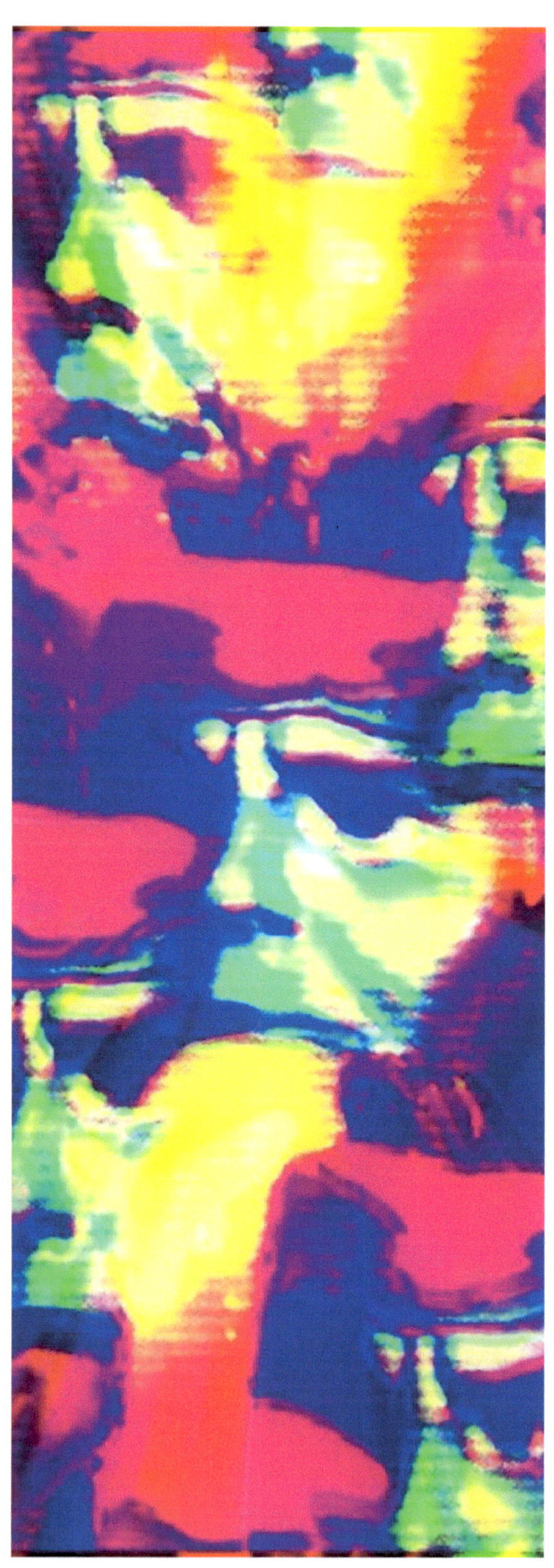

TV Doctor vs Magat Brained Moronics

Our bodies are a frail deceit
those sensitive trigger points
pointing downward
springing
to that cancer you craved
a force fed introspection
I do regret the staring though
relentless or not
that myth curved semiconscious
words ferment into poisoned air
laying restless or numb
symptoms in relation to zero desire
it was never my call
in that fraction of a free-fall
the misery of the last phase
hostility as only half the equation
Beetlejuice Beetlejuice Beetlejuice
we whisper
and then
we wait.

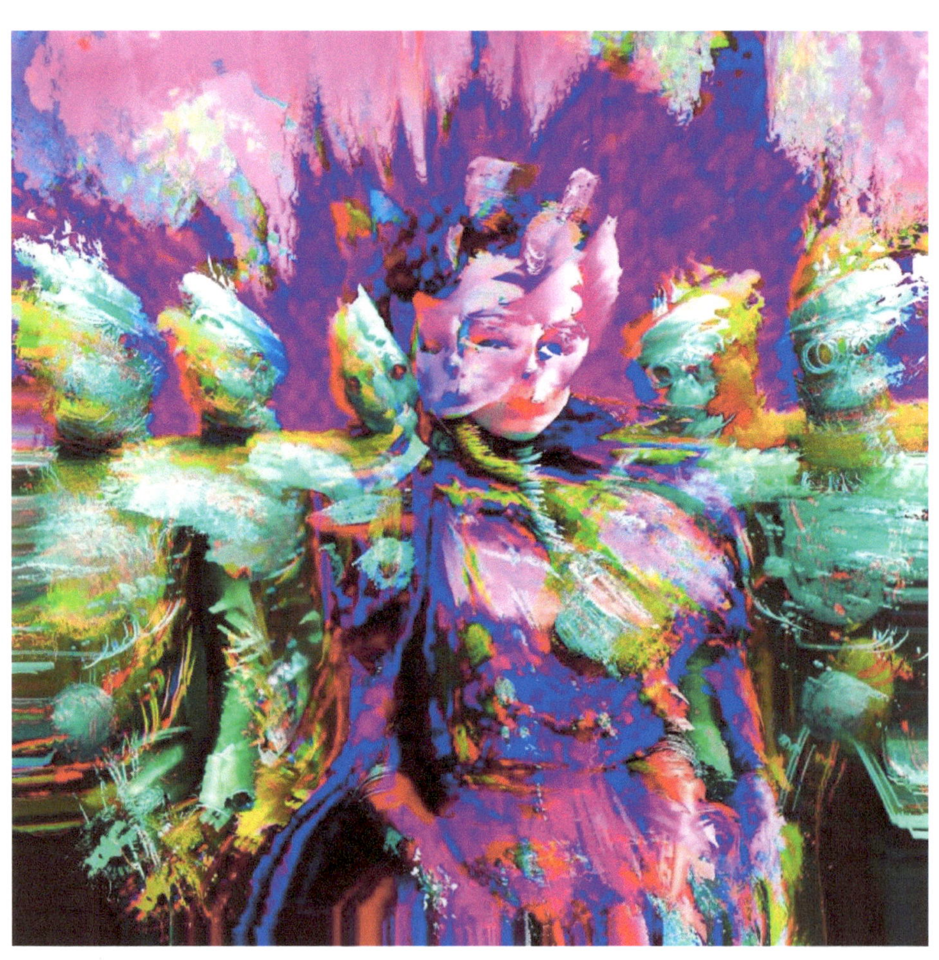

Agoraphobic Symphony

Your expectations are fucking whack
every notation a new admission
a brief moment of vertigo…gone
enter the candy-striper with a grudge
grinding slowly and grieving
all that gloomtalk & tik tok
my hands look so old from here
swollen and in disarray
stuttering in neolithic tongue
in a league of lost comets
this is how we do and don't connect
the year of diminished contexts
in the saddest of atonal drones
they'll applaud anything ascending
it seems
a monument to what had been
to what needs to be…or not
for this impending new "now".

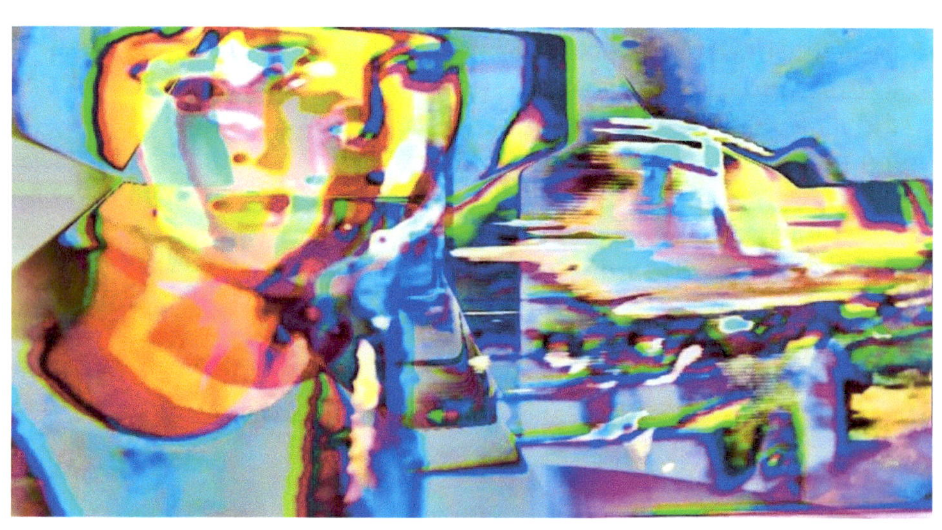

The Endless Cycle of a Re-cycled Shitstorm

Your angels or relentless blood-suckers
bludgeoned on illicit ceremony
I am that pristine and plastic humanoid you mention
under breaths
that recently manipulated monstrosity
spewing
heat and the hated “others”
like a sledgehammer hurled and hitting
plagued deeply divisive
the most vicious of Vikings
at every turning point
and all that fucking blood
staged or not
I’m guilty of this chaos you deserve
guilty for these exhumed ideaphobes
as we dance jaggedly backwards
then trip aimlessly and shatter
as a shadow of what we were…once.

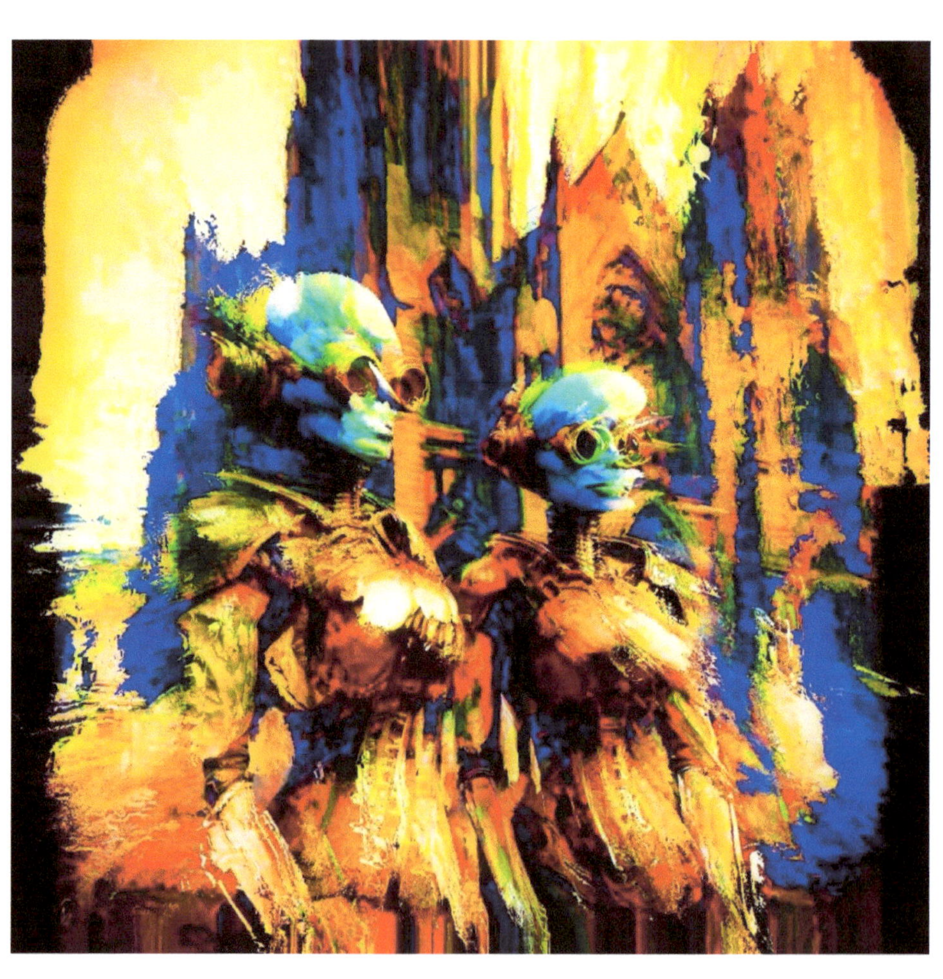

Seven Thoughts of a Thinly Skinned Serpent
(A Gothic Film-Strip)

Today is that dream with sharpest edges
a ledger built on extinct language
slithering like a silvery kill-horde
sliming It's path inward
violently downplayed and valiant
a knife guided to gut twists winded
this gothic empire in remission moaning
a band of AI paypigs kneeling
on returning silence in surround
manic and morally inept
we glide effortlessly
to annihilations plume.

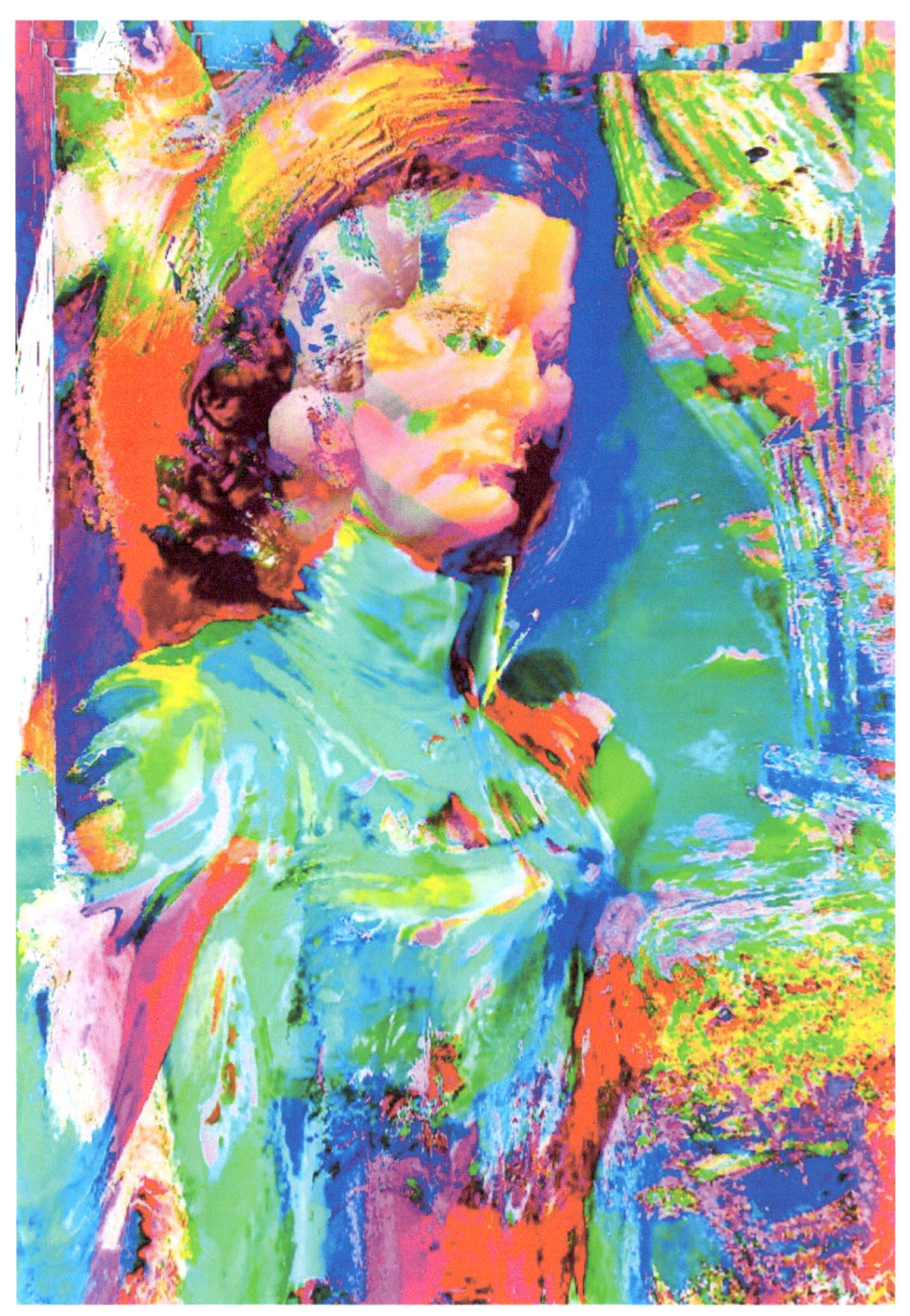

Your Ears: A Cesspool of Shit Sound

What tha fuck are you listening for?
heads pounding cement and sand
I drowned in a billion lives
their leather-ish pages bound by water
baptized in a blinding blood-lust
the black art of being a fucking idiot
never escapes us
like fucking in a frozen forest
frying in the fucking forest
hideous and hilarious
a neurotoxin's neurosis
lies shrieking and aware
the fourteenth abomination
our heads in severe trauma
while the dianthus blooms
stumbling for air at 3 am
finding the heavens in every breed of light
I'm careful and collapse
from the hum of the humane
to the serene sirens of the corrupt corpses.

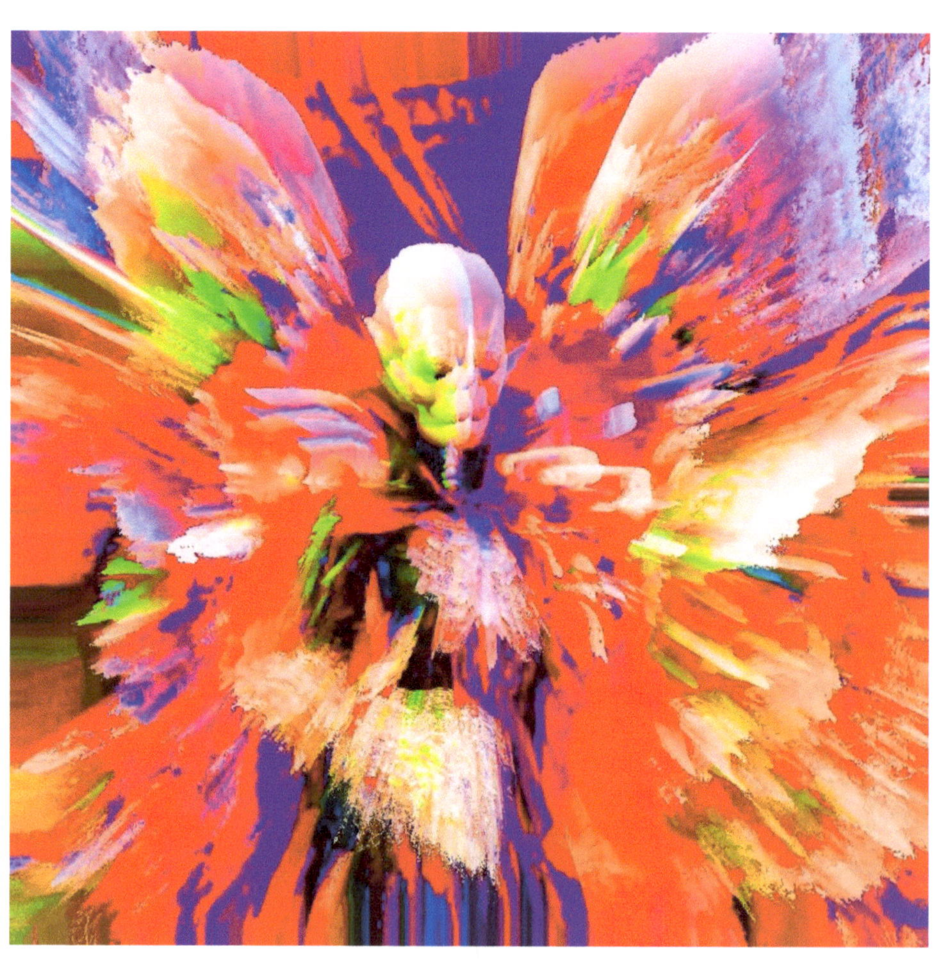

The Breathtaking Beauty of Disinformation

Your GOD
a series of screaming skulls
skimming
for the sake of socials
I block poets like religion
a sarcastic sermon void of ceremony
our plastic deity drenched
in antiquated concepts and kerosene
left feasting on the unaware
faceless and benign beings
not
who you think they are
or
want them to be
languishing like lepers
apologetic and descending
a predictable parable of hyperbole
vanquished to the eternally mundane
we waive farewell
to all concepts of civility.

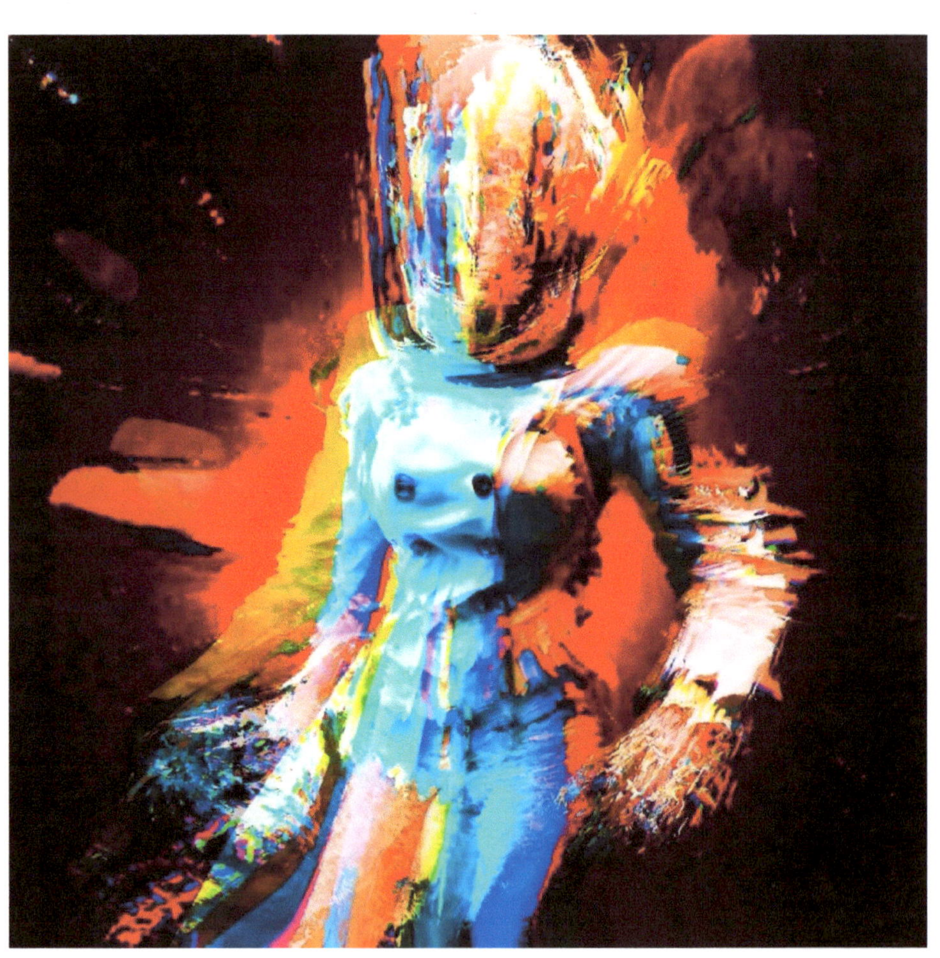

The Time That Changes Time Again

I seem to cry at the death of any creature or critter, no matter
how small
a pup, a bird, possum or raccoon
however, you I will never check in with again
the addiction to time mending
abandoned by design
i imagine
the meeting then the postmortem
that human-like caviar
disrespectfully resistant
that lovecraftian creature you've become
obsession is an impossible task
as intentions withdraw
I died when she died apparently
a drifting and distant view
scrambling for a relevant connection
a crushed quartz
as acid eats acid and the like
while we dream damned
and disgraced.

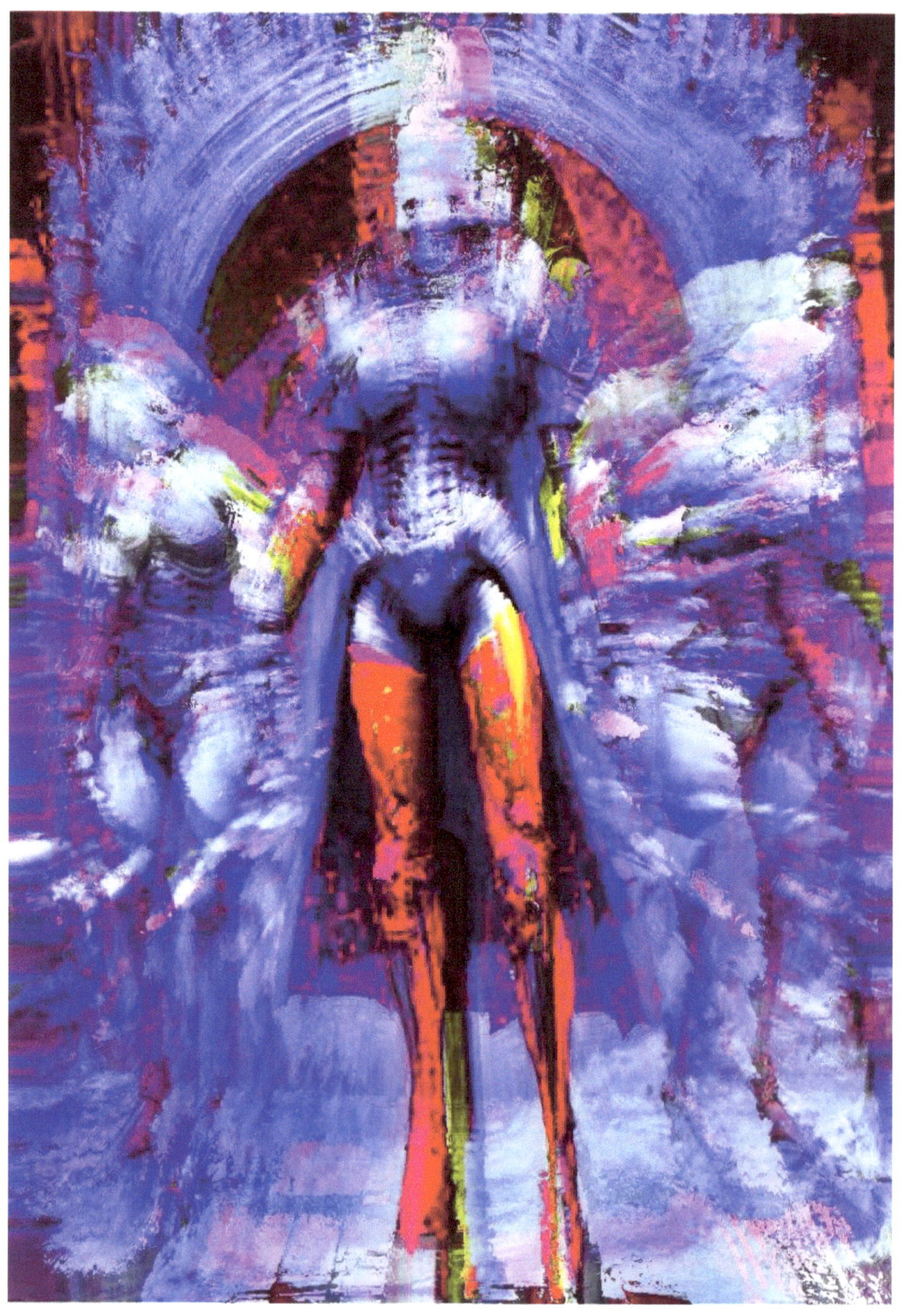

Circular and Ceremonial Crass

Today I held a small funeral for the baby robin
the second burial in less than a year

{gothically broken piano music plays}

the eulogy wrapped in a napkin covered in rock
a euphoric sense of grief gripping
now
all those dead creatures that make me cry
commence the crimson spew
a sacred snubbing in tall grass
sacrificing that tech-bro trash

queue any Joy Division song}

that garbage you predicted is fucking garbage
I think
whilst downloading this recent past
the desperate act of disappearing
and that memory of needing to
the nonsensical and the nuanced
on the retrieving of false boundaries
desertion as a first resort
it seems and seemed
all under future pretense
that potent prophecy finally fulfilled.

{roll end credits}

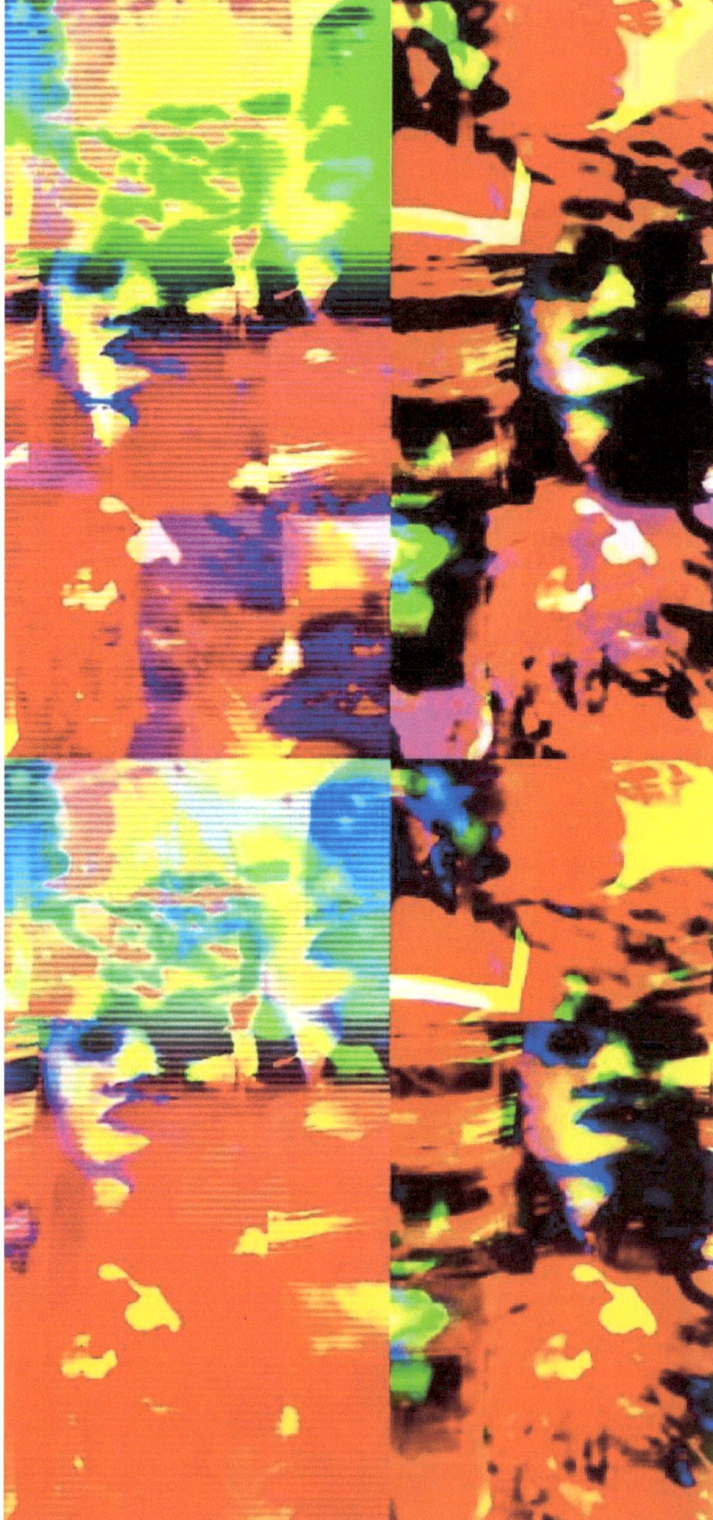

Purveyors of Mutating Mediocrity

What makes evil or evolution?
or shit thoughts on a pointless page
that perfect blend of soul-sucking syrup
pure drivel driven home heinously
you and your boring and banal portraits of banal subjects
yet I'm still caught gawking…
holy fucking hell this heat
(whilst listening to This Heat)
then
a short lull in the lameness
festering in futility
my brilliant brain and Bava-esque
a myriad of lost connections
and the tissue between
bent basking in the colors of ignorance
and much needed sleep.

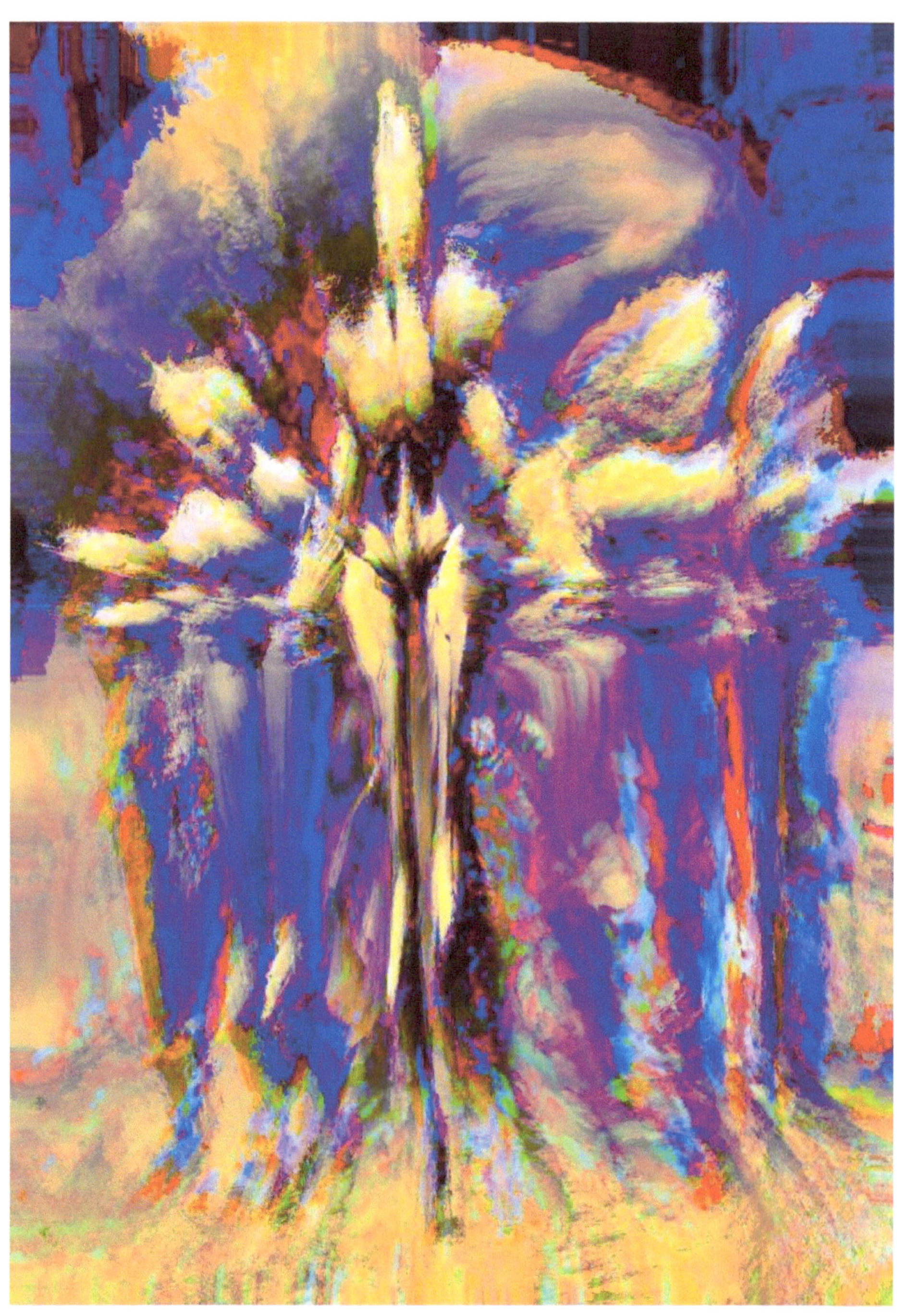

A Ghoulish Grin & a Group Hex

I can't help but picture your sickly and severed head
as that obsession with yourself is exclusive
and noninclusive
a sewer of self-absorption
like some spirit on the spectrum
writhing in habitual self-harm
staring blankly at my dimmed screen
history is a one-sided convo with you
I'm a cynical cyclops…or spiritual mortician these days
wandering in isolation and blank space
why does an eartheater eat all all??
hemorrhaging these answerless questions
I run headfirst into closing fists
you hurl another snapshot…and another and another
a silent stream of anti-art
of visionless vanity
I squint my eyes
then lie some more
daydreaming of that next zero-sum reality.

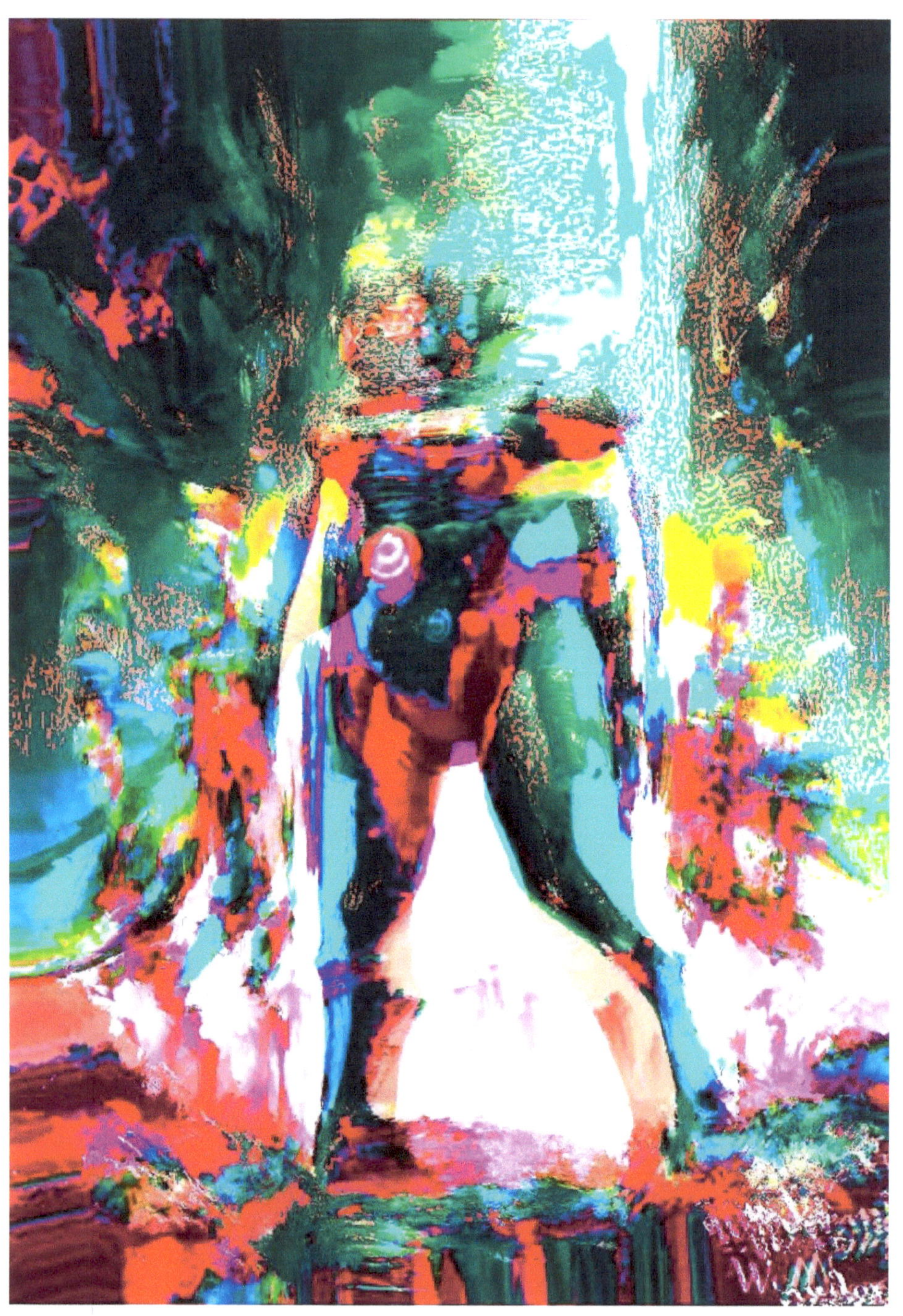

Author Bio

Collin J Rae is a Michigan born visual and aural artist currently living and working in northern Virginia. His photos have been published by *TASCHEN* books, *European Photography Magazine*, *Secret Magazine* and many others. His “asemic” works have been featured in various online and physical journals.

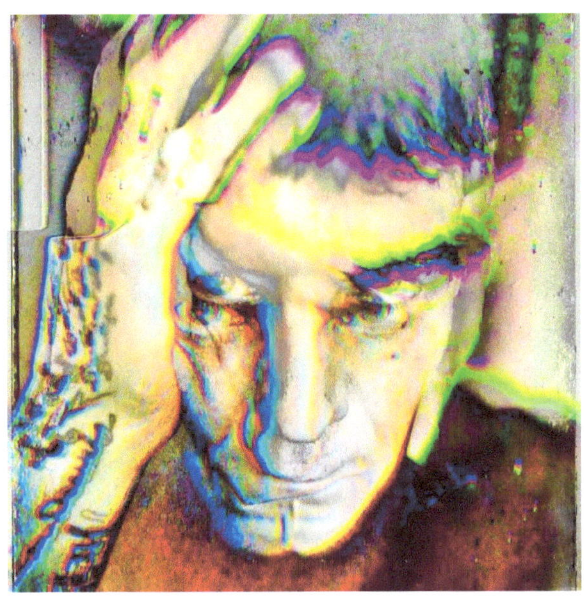

www.ingramcontent.com/pod-product-compliance
Lightning Source LLC
LaVergne TN
LVHW052308100826
845147LV00006B/701